T0195900

SEXUAL CRIMES
IN AFRICA AND HOW TO DEAL WITH THEM

ZAMBIA AND SIX OTHER AFRICAN COUNTRIES IN PERSPECTIVE

FUNSO

authorHOUSE®

AuthorHouse™
1663 Liberty Drive
Bloomington, IN 47403
www.authorhouse.com
Phone: 1 (800) 839-8640

Published by AuthorHouse 12/30/2019

ISBN: 978-1-7283-4095-1 (sc)
ISBN: 978-1-7283-4094-4 (e)

CONTENTS

FOREWORD

It was at first a pleasant shock for me, when I received notification, from the learned and erudite author, to write a foreword to this book, on the vexed subject of sexual offences. The menace of sexual offences, which in themselves are birthed through the rising cases of sexual immorality within the society, must be tamed and buried, through education, enlightenment and deliberate campaigns, such as offered by this book.

The world is currently ensconced in sexual violence, sexual abuses and sexual assaults, all manifesting in constant rape cases, shocking reports of defilements, bestiality and lately, incest and very unnatural sexual intercourse. On the surface, it would seem that there are no statutory remedies, or that extant legislative efforts are inadequate, to tackle these monstrous developments.

In this rare expose, the author has made an unusual but bold foray into the jurisprudence of sexual offences, tracing their origin and root causes, analyzing and dissecting the relevant legislations and also proffering solutions to curb the rising menace. The knowledge and research that have gone into producing this book are very profound indeed, given the learned author's varied assignments. The learned author, through this book, traversed the continent of Africa, using The Republic of Zambia, as a case study, combining his legal proficiency with superb spiritual analysis, of the issues, thus offering a balanced perspective, into the causes, effects and curtailment of sexual crimes.

The book started with a historical survey of the basic elements of crime, that is actus reus and mens rea and then journeyed, most profoundly, into the mode of crime, the parties involved, the peculiarity of the offences of rape, defilement, incest and other unnatural intercourse. The author then surveyed the methodology and strategy of the law enforcement agencies, highlighting the novel efforts of the Victim Support Unit (VSU) and proffering very useful suggestions, on the way forward.

The learned author's clinical dissection of section 21 of the Penal Code of Zambia, gives a vivid lucidation of the ingredients of most sexual offences, such that will assist both the prosecution and indeed the defense, in dealing with incidents of sexual offences, either in the police station or in court.

In the light of the seeming confusion that the whole world has now been thrown into by proponents and activists of unnatural sexual misconducts, the book presents an inspiring rescue from the universal dose of passivity.

The courage to speak and be counted as a credible alternative to the almost pervasive sexual dysfunction currently prevailing is most commendable, more so in the way the learned author has, in his characteristic simplicity, offered very elementary expositions, that can be followed, even by non-lawyers.

I wholeheartedly recommend this piece, as a jurisprudential classic, on the topic of sexual offences, that should adorn public and private libraries and such that should be adopted in all schools where law is taught and indeed as a working tool, for all prosecutors, defense counsel and judicial officers alike.

PREFACE

This inquisition is borne out of an outcry from citizens about sexual crimes, namely: Rape, Defilement and Incest that are rampant. The Analyst, using his experience as a seasoned Victim Support Officer, tries to bring out these offences in this inquest.

The idea of the Analyst is to dig deep onto what the Zambian Penal Code (Chapter 87 of the Laws of Zambia) says about sexual crimes and how to deal with these crimes. This inquest also will look at various judgements of the courts, ranging from Zambian to British judgements, as well as judgements from other Commonwealth countries.

It will also attempt to include sexual crimes Acts of Botswana, Kenya, Malawi, South Africa, Nigeria and Zimbabwe. In its analysis, the research will try to bring out the law concerning sexual crimes to the doorstep of the reading public. Once people understand the law, the prevention of sexual offences will be easy. This will also have added effect of preserving lives through reduction of cases of HIV/AIDS. To preserve life is the most important objective of every institution.

The Author eventually also suggests the review and amendment of old laws as well as enactment of new ones, to meet contemporary challenges and he believes various Penal Codes have deficiencies which parliaments should deal with urgently.

INTRODUCTION

Cri m i n a l l i a b i l i t y i s b a s e d u p o n a combination of actions, (actus reus) thoughts and mind set (mens rea). This is expressed by the maxim actus non facit reum nisi mens sit rea, which means that an act alone will not give rise to criminal liability unless it was done with a guilty state of mind (Emily Flinch et al 2009:2). If actus reus and mens rea are established and there is no valid defence, the defendant is guilty. The onus or burden of proofs is on the prosecution to establish the elements of the offence beyond reasonable doubt. This is required to e s t a b l i s h c r i m i n a l l i a b i l i t y (s t a n d a r d o f proof) (Emily Flinch et al 2009:2). It is the responsibility of Government to protect its citizens from all forms of criminal activities. Hence it has enacted Laws, usually adopted from the British Laws, in order to achieve this objective, the enforcement of which is achieved through law e n f o r c e m e n t. L a w e n f o r c e m e n t S e r v i c e Headquarters and their officers enforce these laws.

The objectives of the Laws of every country are to:

  i.   preserve life
  ii. Protect property
  iii. Prevent the commission of crime and detect offenders who commit crime
  iv. Keep the peace among citizens

The Zambian criminal law is enshrined in the Penal Code. The objectives of the Penal Code, among others, are:

i. To sound a fair warning to citizens who might commit offences; to warn citizens with criminal properties.
ii. To act as a guide in matters of criminal trespass.
iii. To distinguish between misdemeanors and felonies and offer respective sentences.
iv. To deter misconducts that threaten or inflict harm on human life.
v. To punish offenders

The officers of laws and Police officers are properly taught how to use the Penal Code when enforcing the law. However, the major difficulty the officers encounter is that the Penal Code has not been frequently amended, hence, there is very little difference contained therein that distinguishes it from the Northern Rhodesia Penal Code. As such, certain conduct prevailing in Zambia, that constitute offences in other countries, are not recognized by Parliament as crimes, for example, indecent exposure.

Various Zambian and British cases, and those from other Commonwealth countries have been used as reference cases and binding precedents. In this work, unless stated therein, is the accused person and is the actual perpetrator of the crime. B is a principal offender or second accused and can be an aider, abettor, counselor or procurer. C is the complainant and can be the victim e.g. in rape cases, it is the person actually raped, or a relative to the victim e.g. mother reporting on behalf of a daughter in a defilement case.

Other letters, like D, E, O, P, X, Y, Z, etc., can be replaced with names.

CHAPTER 1

Parties to sexual offences

Funso

Parties To Sexual Crimes

Crimes falling into the "sex crimes" category generally involve illegal or coerced sexual conduct by one person towards another. There are laws against unlawful sexual conduct in every state, and each state has its own time limit to bring a sexual—related lawsuit. People convicted of sex crimes are considered "sex offenders" by the state and face having their names added to state and federal sex offenders registers? Below is a collection of crimes that are sexual in nature, and that carry severe consequences and penalties.

An offence is said to be committed when a person does some illegal acts that injure the society in general (Schmalleger F 2013:109). Many people believe that the actual perpetrator of a crime is the only person liable for criminal proceedings. This is not true, as the courts and parliament have realized that criminal liability should not only be placed on the actual offender but also on others who, though they did not actively participate in the commission of the crime, played a part.

These people who are parties to offences are called principal offenders. Police officers follow Section 21 of the Penal Code in enforcing this law. When a complaint is received, after interviewing the victim, officers determine which people to summon or apprehend and interrogate, and if possible arrest them as principal offenders.

Section 21 states ways in which a person can be a principal offender.

Acts and omissions of an offence

In criminal law (Schmalleger F, 2013:103), an offence can be committed by doing an act or making an omission. An act has more to do with conduct in offences like rape, defilement, incest, etc. An omission has more to do with negligence of an individual (Schm-allege-r F·2-013:1·04).

That is to say, where a person knows that it is his or her duty to do certain jobs but fails to do them, or knowing that he or she has a legal duty to prevent the commission of a crime, but fails to act and offence has been committed. For example, it is the duty of every parent or guardian to care for a child; any parent failing to do so commits an omission offence of neglecting to provide necessities (food, clothing, etc.) for such a child.

Equally, every person has a duty, where it is within his or her means, to prevent the commission of homicide. In short, every Zambian has the duty to preserve life and failure to do so, makes one to commit an omission offence of neglect to prevent commission of a felony. Hence, it is just in order to arrest a medical doctor for murder, when knowing that his wife is sick but fails to attend to her.

Definition of a crime or an offence

Various scholars and judges have defined a crime or an offence in many ways. Though familiar to the lay person, the terms 'murder' and 'rape' also carry fairly precise legal messages to the lawyer. In their legal contexts, these terms build in considerations which not only filter out the insane perpetrator but also confine their scope to those who act in some criminally blameworthy fashion. According to Mason A (1995, 4 *Griffith LR 147),* conduct described in terms like 'causing injury' does not necessarily deserve criminalization, even if there is no unusual feature such as insanity about the case. The injury may have been caused directly or indirectly, intentionally or by accident, carelessly or without fault. All or any of these factors may be relevant to the question of whether the lawyer or the non-lawyer considers the conduct as criminal.

Both lawyers and others readily recognize that breaches of some of the Ten Commandments warrant criminal sanction. But there is room for considerable difference between the criminal law and this version of God's law. While murder, perjury and theft are prohibited by the Ten Commandments and criminal law alike, the world over, adultery is prohibited by the seventh commandment but not by the criminal law in Zambia. Yet, in some societies adultery is not only regarded as a crime, but as a very serious crime.

Under Islamic law, for instance, adultery could be punished by death by stoning (MansourA: 1982 p199). This is not to say that this is the law in most Islamic countries for instance, Turkey has recently decriminalized adultery. Adultery was also, according to Blackstone (64-65), a capital offence in the English Commonwealth period, and a crime in most American States (Weinstein JD, 1987:225), and remains a crime in Utah (Kearney J, 1994:70). However, a crime or an offence may be defined as a legal wrong-doing that can either be an act or omission, or both, and it is punishable by the court of law.

On the surface, to ask "what is a crime?" seems to warrant a straightforward answer in that one can simply suggest that "crime is something that is against the law." For those who adopt such a strict definition, or a legal—consensus approach to crime, for example Tappan 1947, studying the law as it is written is sufficient for understanding what society considers harmful behaviour. However, if we take a step back from this literal interpretation to consider the broader social processes that help give meaning to crime and its control, it quickly becomes apparent that there is much more to the question than simply referring to what is written in the law. As Comack and Brickey (1991, 15) remind us,"[l] law can be said to have a distinctly *social basis*; it both shapes – and is shaped by – the society in which it operates" (emphasis in the original). Indeed, before a criminal statute is even contemplated, there are a whole host of social forces and events that both shape how we conceive of a particular behaviour and influence our decisions on how to respond. In addition, many of these social forces continue to shape our response strategies well after the social wrong becomes part of our legal lexicon. How society thinks about crime and the individuals deemed to be responsible for criminal behaviour influences law e n f o r c e m e n t p r a c t i c e s a n d t h e p e n a l t i e s administered. Why is it that certain behaviour is deemed sufficiently problematic to warrant being labelled a crime?

Analysis of Section 21

A person can be accused of committing an offence if: a. he or she actually does the act or makes an omission that constitutes an offence.

Meaning that, he is the actual perpetrator of the crime either by doing the act or omitting to do the right thing.

If A attacks and rapes C whilst B, a friend of A, is watching and does nothing to help in the prevention of the offence of rape, both of them are offenders. A is the primary offender since he actually did the act. Whilst B is a secondary offender since he omitted to prevent its commission, and can be found guilty of rape unless he can prove that he had no means of stopping A from raping C. If, suppose, both A and B ended up having sex with C without her consent, then they both raped C.

b. he or she makes the commission of the crime easier or possible by assisting the primary offender during the commission of the crime.

If A attacks C in an attempt to rape her, but C is too strong to be overpowered by A and B offers assistance by holding her hands as A rapes her, A is the actual perpetrator of a crime and is guilty of rape whilst B is a principal offender since he assisted the actual perpetrator. If B did not assist, A couldn't have committed the crime of rape. Instead, he could have been guilty of attempted rape or indecent assault. Section 21(b) extends as well to men and women who may provide a bedroom or a house so that their friend can easily rape a woman.

C. he or she makes the commission of a crime possible by aiding or abetting. Section 21(c) can be divided into 21(c) (i) – aiding and 21(c) (ii) – as abetting. Section 21(c) (I) –aiding.

To aid is to give help or assistance to an activity.

Therefore, an aider is one who helps or assists another during the commission of the crime. For one to be an aider, he must be present at the scene or be at a reasonable distance from the scene. Also, it must be understood that mere presence at the scene without aiding the perpetrator does not constitute an offence.

For example, X may go to visit C and upon arrival, he hears C screaming for help as she is being raped. Sooner or later, police officers arrive and apprehend A, the rapist and X, alleging that they were together. X cannot be arrested as he never aided or abetted in the commission of the crime despite the fact that he was present at the scene.

B is an aider if, when A is raping C, he or she is watching at a distance to see if people are coming. He is also an aider if he covers C's mouth so that she does not scream.

Section 21 (c) (ii)—abetting

To abet is to encourage or incite, at the time of the offence. To incite is to encourage somebody to do something illegal, violent or unpleasant, especially by making someone angry or excited. For one to be an abettor he or she must be present at the scene of crime.

B is an abettor if he encourages A, e.g. with words like 'even if she screams just go ahead and have sex with her'. B also commits an offence if he incites A, for example, like saying: 'If you fail to sleep with her then you are not a man.

"How can a woman overpower you? It means you are not man enough.'

'It is a sign of impotence if you are already on top of a woman then you fail to have sex with her.

'If you can't remove her underwear, just push it the other side.'

Such are incitement comments and they constitute an offence.

d. he or she counsels or procures another person to commit the crime.

To counsel is to encourage or incite before the commission of the offence. The only difference between counsel and abet is the time when one is deemed to have incited or abetted the primary offender. Encouragement or incitement during the commission of a crime is abetting. Counselling also involves planning of how the offence shall be committed.

B will be deemed to have counseled A if, he or she helps or shows or plans with A, how A should commit a crime against C. For example, a traditional doctor who advises A, a 45-year-old man, to sleep with a 3-year-old girl in order for him to get cured of HIV/AIDS or become rich, is a counselor who should be arrested for defilement should A defile the girl.

Also, if A, a 19-year-old young man, who has never had sex before constantly admires C, his sister-in—law, but fails to propose to her because she is an underage – 14 years old. A seeks advice from his cousin B. B advises A what to do in order to have sex with C. She tells A that he should just call C to his bedroom, kiss her and then force her into sex. If she tries to scream, he should cover her mouth with the hand. If A does what B told him and rapes C, B will be guilty of counseling.

To procure is to cause a particular effect by making every effort. In order to procure an offence, there must be causation of the same offence. That is to say, there must be a relationship between what the procurer does and the offence committed and that the procurer made every effort to cause the commission of the offence and see desired results.

In our judgement, it is irrelevant that the man whom Leak procured to do the physical act himself did not intend to have sexual intercourse with the wife without her consent. Leak was using him as a means to procure a criminal purpose.

An accused, who aids and abets another man to have intercourse with a woman knowing that she does not consent, may be found guilty of aiding and abetting rape, notwithstanding that the other man is acquitted of rape on the ground that he mistakenly believed that the woman was consenting. It is immaterial that the accused is the woman's husband.

If we are right in our opinion that the wife had been raped (and no one outside a court of law would say that she had not been), then the particulars of the offence stated what Leak had done, namely, he procured Cogan to commit an offence. This would suffice to uphold his conviction.

It can be seen that the belief by some people that only the actual perpetrator of a sexual offence, be it rape or defilement, is to bear a harsh sentence, whilst an aider or an abettor or a procurer or a counselor gets a lesser sentence is not true. Also, as it shall be seen in DPP v. Morgan, Morgan was given a harsh sentence as compared to the tree young men he procured to ravish his wife additionally, the principle of innocent agents is one thought by some people to apply only to cases like theft, murder, etc. For example, if B gives poison to E, his 18—year-old son to give to D his wife, on pretext that the same is a drug to cure diarrhea that D is suffering from and eventually D dies as a result of the administered poison, E is an innocent agent to murder for he never knew that what he gave to D was poison to kill her. Therefore it is B to be arrested for murder. Even in rape, innocent agents like Cogan, can be found as long as facts show that the woman consented or was consenting.

A woman cannot commit rape or defilement, but she can be a principal offender. As such if she procures rape by use of either force or any other means on another woman or a girl, such that a woman or a girl submits to sexual intercourse with a man, the man strongly and without doubt believing that the woman is consenting, then it is right that the principle in Cogan and Leak apply to her.

For a person to be accused of counseling or procuring, the person counseled must commit the alleged counseled crime or, the crime must be committed by the person procured to do it. An attempt to counsel or procure does not constitute an offence. If the counselor wishes to change his or her mind about the advice given, he is still liable as an accessory if, before he communicates with the counselee, the offence counseled is committed.

Additionally, Section 23 of the Penal Code on counseling another to commit an offence states as follows:

When a person counsels another to commit an offence, and an offence is actually committed after such counsel by the person to whom the counsel is given: it is immaterial:

(a) Whether the offence actually committed is the same as that counseled or a different one.

For example, A seeks help from B on how to rape C, a 17—year-old girl. B advises A to use force and to cover her mouth so that she does not scream. A manages to have sex with C by force, but during the act, since his right hand covered her mouth and nose, C suffocates and dies. When A is charged with murder, B also will be charged with murder and he cannot use the defense of having counseled A to rape C only and not to kill her.

Difference in offence committed does not protect B from being convicted.

(b) Or, whether the offence is committed in the way counseled or in a different way. For example, B counsels A to have sexual intercourse with C by adding a sleeping tablet to her drink. A consents to B's advice, but when he meets C, he threatens her with a gun and she submits to his demands. After sex, she reports him for rape. B has also to be arrested as an accessory before the fact.

Provided in either (a) and (b) the facts constituting the offence actually committed are a probable consequence of carrying out the counsel. In either case, the person who gave the counsel is deemed to have counseled the other person to commit the offence actually committed by him. A non-sexual offence, which is the best example, is that of homicide. If B counsels A to kill D by poisoning and A kills D by stabbing him with a screwdriver, both A and B will have murdered D. B cannot be acquitted on grounds that the way the crime was committed was different from the way he counseled A.

i. **Generally, a crime can be committed by:** the actual perpetrator of a crime, who is also

ii. Referred to as the principal offender.

iii. An accessory before the fact. This is a person

iv. Who may abet or aid or counsel or procure the commission of a crime. He is also called a principal offender. an accessory after the fact. This is a person who knowing that a person has committed a crime harbours him or her, or assists him to escape punishment

So, in the scenario above, MM is the actual perpetrator of a crime. JJ, HT and PR are accessories before the fact, and Mumbi's elder sister is an accessory after the fact, if knowingly that his brother had committed sexual offence, she hides him.

On accessories after the fact, the Penal Code in Section 397 further indicates that a wife cannot be an accessory for the offence committed by her husband. Neither is she liable, if she assists, in her husband's presence and by his authority, another person who has committed an offence together with her husband. Also, a husband does not become an accessory after the fact to an offence of which his wife is guilty by favouring or assisting her in order to enable her to escape.

Punishment of principal offenders

Principal offenders, as outlined in Section 21, are deemed to have committed the offence just like the actual perpetrator of the crime and are charged, tried and sentenced like the actual offender. However the sentence, many times, exercises leniency depending on the role played by each accused person in the commission of a crime

Section 22 of the Penal Code states that:

When two or more persons form a common intention to prosecute an unlawful purpose in conjunction with one another, and in the prosecution of such purpose an offence is committed of such a nature that its commission was probable consequence of the prosecution of such purpose, each of them is deemed to have committed the offence.

Section 22 of the Penal Code states that:

When two or more persons form a common intention to prosecute an unlawful purpose in conjunction with one another, and in the prosecution of such purpose an offence is committed of such a nature that its commission was probable consequence of the prosecution of such purpose, each of them is deemed to have committed the offence.

Such offenders are referred to as joint offenders. For example, if A and B plan to steal from C a television set and radio, and they successfully steal the items in such a way that A breaks into the house and carries the items to the vehicle and drives off whilst B keeps guard so that if people are coming, he alerts A, both of them would have jointly, and whilst acting together, committed the offence of house breaking and theft, regardless of the fact that B did not touch the property stolen or break the Door C

An accessory after the fact of an offence is punished according to Section 398 of the Penal Code which states that:

Any person who becomes an accessory after the fact to a felony is guilty of a felony, and is liable, if no other punishment is provided, to imprisonment for three years.

There has been a lot of argument regarding Section 21, mainly by police officers, as far as sexual offences are concerned. What causes such argument is the fact that officers have increasing access to foreign books on criminal law. These books, mostly from commonwealth countries, emphasize the grading of offenders into first—degree offender, that is, the actual perpetrator of the crime, and second-degree offender, that is, an aider or abettor or counselor or procurer. Some of these books contain precedents that indicate that abettors, aiders, procurers and counselors of rape or defilement should not be charged with rape or defilement like the actual perpetrator.

The other confusing part of the law comes in when officers are looking at the composite of the definition of the offence and the benefits accruing to the perpetrator. For example, to prove rape, there must be: unlawful penetration, sexual intercourse and without a woman's consent. So, if one of these ingredients is missing then there is no rape committed. The act of sex may be unlawful but the woman consented. Also, there may be penetration without consent, but the act turns out not to be rape because unlawfulness is absent. For example, a man having sex with a fast sleeping wife does so by using the implied consent that he obtained when he married her but the daily express of consent is missing.

The benefit of sex is to enjoy the act. So, how can an accessory before the fact be arrested for rape when he never penetrated the woman? It is argued that whilst there are benefits in other cases accruing to accessories, for example in theft the benefit is to share the stolen property; in a treason case, the benefit is to share power; in a rape case, there are no benefits accruing to an accessory.

The foreign law on sexual offences conflicts with the Zambian legislation. However, it is clear that where there is a conflict between the foreign law and the Zambian Law, the Zambian legislature prevails. Therefore, Section 21 is applicable to all offences. Unless the Penal Code has another offence for the accessory, an accused can be charged as the actual perpetrator. For example, if A forges a cheque and gives it to B for cashing at a bank and later B is apprehended because the cheque is discovered by the teller not to be genuine, A will be arrested for forgery and B for uttering a forged cheque. It does not matter whether A said to B, 'Take this forged cheque and cash it.'

Contrary to the above law, if A steals a radio from C's house at night and tells B to sell it saying, 'Please go and sell this stolen radio, we shall share the money.' Should B get caught, both A and B will be arrested for burglary and theft. Sexual offences are not exempted from Section 21. So, an aider, abettor, procurer or counselor should be charged together with the actual perpetrator of the crime. So, an aider who helped the rapist to separate the legs of the victim should actually be charged with rape. The benefit of an accessory in every offence is either direct or indirect. In sexual offences, there is a direct benefit of helping a friend hence strengthening the relationship. There is also an indirect benefit of seeing a woman or a girl suffer as a result of trauma, as is the case of all who derive some pleasure from the suffering of their victims.

A police officer can turn an aider into a state witness if he or she rendered help to the rapist or defiler under duress.

For example, B may admit that he held the hands of the victim as A raped her. But he may also say that he could not have refused to help as A had threatened to kill him if he did not do so. This is not unusual, especially if the aider is a young person (below 19 years). If C supports B's claim, that indeed he was threatened, it is just in order that B is turned into a state witness so that the evidence is consolidated. Another principal offender who may go free is a counselor, for he may claim that he never counseled the accused to commit a crime.

An abettor cannot go unpunished for he is the one who incites the perpetrator and may be identified by the victim. So, if B shouts at A, 'cover her mouth so that she does not scream; and hurry up people may find us', he or she is just inciting A to rape the woman.

Equally, a procurer is the causal party of the offence and it is difficult for him or her to go unpunished. So, if B, a 40—year-old mother, is a drunkard and likes drinking beer on credit, owes A money which she fails to pay back. And, as a way of paying back some of the credit, she asks A to come home at night and have sex with C, her 15-year-old daughter, and she explains to C that if she refuses to have sex with A, she will be taken to court and get jailed. C, in order to prevent her mother from going to jail, consents to sex with A. B has just procured the commission of defilement.

There is also a provision in the Penal Code that makes offenders in case of rape, defilement and other felonies not to go free. Section 393 states that:

Every person who, knowing that a person designs to commit or is committing a felony, fails to use all reasonable means to prevent the commission or completion thereof, is guilty of a misdemeanour.

According to Section 38, the maximum punishment for misdemeanour is two years. A police officer using his discretion can apply Section 393 to charge an accessory before the fact.

So, if the aider or abettor or counselor or procurer cannot be charged with rape or defilement, they can be charged with neglect to prevent commission of (a felony) rape or neglect to prevent commission of defilement.

Furthermore, defilement has been given additional attention in the Penal Code. Section 150 states that:

Any person who conspires with another to induce any woman or girl, by means of any false pretences or other fraudulent means, to permit any man to have unlawful carnal knowledge of her, is guilty of a felony (termed conspiracy to defile) and is liable to imprisonment for three years.

To conspire is to secretly plan with other people to do something illegal or harmful and false pretence means false representations. The representations can be made by words, writing or conduct. May be, the best is to use deceiving instead of false pretences.

There are times when a lesser crime that the procurer of counselor or abettor or aider expected to occur does not happen, or it happens but beyond his or her expectations. In sexual offences, the common outcome is murder. For example, if A is counseled by B to rape C by threatening C with a knife and A, instead, threatens her with a pistol and accidentally the gun explodes and kills C, both A and B will be charged with murder.

Synopsis

Parties to sexual offences are: (a) The actual perpetrator of the sexual offence. (b) The person who makes commission of the crime easier or possible, e.g. by providing a place (house or bedroom) for rape or defilement. (c) The person present at the scene and who actually helps or encourages the actual perpetrator to commit the crime. (d) A person who actually counseled the perpetrator on how to commit the crime or who procured the crime.

A crime is a legal wrong-doing that can either be an act or commission, or both, and is punishable by the law.

An act has more to do with conduct-offences. Sexual offences are conduct-offences. An omission has to do with negligence of an individual

CHAPTER 2

Elements of a crime

ELEMENTS OF A CRIME

Elements of a crime: actus reus and mens rea.

Once again, a crime may be defined as a legal wrong-doing that can either be an act by Law. oromission, or both, and it is punishable Legal practitioners study criminal law andare conversant with the subject of elements of a crime.

It is not enough, just to know that a crime is an illegal act or omission affecting society, but it is important also to consider what constitute a crime. What constitute a crime are called elements or ingredients of a crime. These elements are very important for they are the ones that determine whether one is guilty of a crime or not. Elements of a crime help the law enforcement agents decide whether to arrest a suspect or not.

It therefore follows that, in criminal law, in many cases a person is not supposed to be arrested and later convicted of a crime, if it cannot be proved beyond reasonable doubt by the prosecution that: (a) the accused caused the crime to occur, or the accused had responsibility over somebody or something but was negligent.

(b) the accused, at the commission of the crime, had a guilty mind.
The causation of the fact or an omission, that is failure in responsibility, is called the actus reus. The guilty mind of the accused is referred to as mens rea of a crime. A person cannot have a guilty mind unless he or she is in the right state of mind. Therefore insane people do not have a right state of mind. As such, they cannot have a guilty mind. They have no mens rea.

The Penal Code, in its definition of offences, mentions the actus reus and the mens rea. Mens rea takes the form of or is expressed in the words like i n t e n t i o n a l l y, k n o w i n g l y, r e c k l e s s n e s s, negligently, malice aforethought, maliciously, etc., whilst the actus reus is described in the definition of the offence and it is in form of conduct.

For example, in rape, consent describes the actus reus of the accused. Mens rea is an intention to have sex with somebody knowing that she does not consent; or recklessness as to whether she has consented or not. In defilement, mens rea is knowledge by the accused that the girl is below 16 or recklessness as to whether a girl is below 16 or not. Whilst actus reus is the conduct of having sexual intercourse with a girl under 16 years by a man.

Many times, when a person commits a crime without the mens rea (intention to do so), such a person has not committed an offence. For example, a person may rape a lady under duress. Though he had sex with her without her giving consent, he cannot be guilty of rape, as he had no intention to do so. If robbers command Ato rape his servant C, threatening to shoot him if he does not do so, A cannot be guilty of rape. Once duress is proved

Therefore, before an accused person is convicted, his or her mental state or element is carefully considered. As a result, the actus reus amounts to a crime only if it is accompanied by the mens rea. Legally, an act only does not make someone guilty of a crime unless his mind is guilty as well, except in case of strictly inability where the state of the mind is immaterial further examination of Actus Reus

The actus reus has got more to do with the conduct of the accused and the consequences of that consequences of that conduct.

Therefore, the actus reus may not necessarily mean an act or omission.

As earlier discussed, in rape. (i) is consent the actus reus? or the sexual intercourse itself—the act of sex? (ii) Does consent or absence of it not deal only with defence? Hence, absence of consent constitutes rape in that the accused person's conduct was not acceptable to the complainant. Even if, it has been emphasized that the elements of a crime: actus reus and mens rea, are profound phrases in criminal law, there are certain circumstances, where, one of the elements is lacking and yet a person is convicted of a crime.

In cases where one element is lacking, actus reus, many times, takes supremacy. Therefore, it follows that absence of the actus reus of a particular crime, even if mens rea is present, means that a crime is not committed. If A intends to force C into sex, but C without realizing that A intends to use force on her, whole heartedly consents before A applies force, his act cannot amount to rape even if he may be scared that he has forced somebody into sex. In this case, the intention (mens rea) to rape is present in A's mind but his conduct (actus rea), which he had hoped would be resisted, was however welcomed by C.

Equally, if A has sex with his girlfriend C with her consent when he believes she is below 16 years old, he may be convinced that he has committed defilement, but if she tells him that she just turned 16, he has not committed an offence of defilement.

It is also argued that, if the actus reus of a crime involves an act, that act should be proved to have been willed by the accused. Generally, an act that is not willed does not constitute an offence. This has to do with accidents or, to be more legal, <u>mistakes of facts are some of the exception.</u>

More on Mens Rea

Mens rea, as earlier stated, is the state of mind that makes a person to act or a failure to comply with a certain code of conduct. Mens rea is the guilty state of mind, or mental element of the accused. An insane person, though having performed the necessary actus reus to commit a crime, commits no offence because his mind is not in the right state. If A, a mad man attacks C and rapes her, he will have committed no offence.

Another exemption, are children.

There are certain circumstances when both the actus reus and mens rea are present yet a person is not guilty of an offence. This is because the accused has a valid defense. For example, killing in self—defense and protection of property. For where else can a man run to if he is attacked at his own house? Nowhere! <u>But the rule of proportionality, consent or absence of it, does not deal only with defense.</u>

In the same way, a woman about to be raped, if she is viciously attacked and she is able to defend herself, she would use such reasonable and minimum force to resist and overcome that of the assailant. If in doing so, the man immediately or thereafter dies, she has not committed murder.

Synopsis

In order to prove that a sexual offence occurred, elements of a crime need to be proved. These are actus reus and mens rea.

Actus reus is the causation of the crime. (a) In rape, consent describes the actus reus.Absence of consent constitutes rape in that the accused's conduct was not welcomed by the complainant. (b) In defilement, actus reus is the conduct of having intercourse with a girl under 16 years.

Mens rea is the guilty state of mind which is expressed through words like repeatedly, intentionally, knowingly, recklessness, etc.

(a) In rape, mens rea is the intention to have sex with a woman or girl knowing that she does not consent or recklessness as to whether or not she has consented or not.

(b) In defilement, mens rea is the knowledge by a man that a girl is below 16 or recklessness as to whether or not a girl is below 16.

CHAPTER 3

Rape

Issues covered

RAPE

The Background Of Consensual Intercourse

To an average Zambian, rape is only committed when a man uses physical force to overpower a woman or girl and have intercourse with her. This idea of understanding consent originates from traditional beliefs. Traditionally, 'yes' to a love proposal symbolized by word of mouth, was to stand still, look down and remain silent. Then the man knew that his proposal was accepted. Those who said 'no' simply walked away and uttered words like: I don't want; I am not interested in sex before marriage; if you want me, it is better you talk to my grandmother, etc. If a young man only wanted sex from a girl, then there was no way he would go and talk to the girl's relatives. Young men and girls were not expected to play together or visit each other, so it was very difficult to propose love to a girl and later on have sex, but when an opportunity presented itself, those who had girlfriends would have sex with them. At the time of intercourse, a man never negotiated for sex, he just told her, mostly by his conduct touching her breasts, waist, etc.), that he wanted to have sex. He then held her very closely and before sex, a girl was expected to show some resistance. The girl's pretentious resistance did not mean non-consent to sexual intercourse but was an indication that she was not an easy girl and it was well understood by a man. As long as a girl never shouted but showed feeble resistance, the man continued to use minimum force until she gave in. Sexual intercourse usually took place in the bush when girls went to draw water or to fetch firewood or at night in the hut of the girl.

This was very risky and was done by naughty girls—girls who did not respect the teaching of: 'be a virgin till marriage'—because a girl was always safeguarded. Very few girls were involved in premarital sex.

That is the traditional background of sexual intercourse in Zambia which, unfortunately, has a lot of influence on modern men and girls. If what used to happen was normal by then, it is no longer normal today. Today we can refer to it as rape, because a 'yes' to a love proposal does not mean yes to sexual intercourse. If a man wants to have sex with his girlfriend, he must ask for it. But unfortunately, young men are taught by older men not to ask a girl for sex, as she would always say no and if she readily accepts then she is not a decent girl. Girls who have had sex, upon being asked for it, have said that they did not expect their boyfriend to have sex with them. They say, they just felt his hands on their breasts and when they tried to resist, he overpowered them by pressing them onto the bed or the carpet. And if asked why they did not report, they claim that their friends advised them not to, as that is how men have sex with girls.

We can now see that due to the bad background of sexual intercourse in Zambia, a lot of work need to be done to educate an ordinary Zambian on what constitutes rape, especially what sexual consent is.

The Legal Definition Of Rape

Rape is a felony. A felony is a serious offence affecting society or the public in general. None—serious offences are called misdemeanors. Rape, defilement, unnatural offences, indecent assaults and incest, are all felonies

The legal definition of rape is contained in Section
132 of the Penal Code.
Section 132: The legal definition of rape

Any person who has unlawful carnal knowledge of a woman or girl without her consent or with her consent, if the consent is obtained by:

(a) Force, or
(b) Means of threats or intimidation of any kind, or
(c) By fear of bodily harm, or
(d) by means of false representation as to the nature of the act, or
(e) in case of married woman by personating her husband, is guilty of a felony termed 'rape'.

Any person who commits the offence of rape is liable to imprisonment for life. (As amended by No. 26 of 1933 and No. 20 of 1964).

The above definition is difficult to understand by laymen in law. Therefore a simple definition of rape that can easily be understood by anyone is:

Rape is when a man has unlawful sexual intercourse with a woman or girl without her consent. It is also rape if a woman or girl consents to sexual intercourse, as long as that consent is obtained:

(a) by force
(b) by means of threats or intimidation of any kind
(c) by fear of bodily harm
(d) by means of false representation as to the nature of the act
(e) and in case of a married woman by personating her husband

Carnal knowledge means sexual intercourse and it includes even the slightest penetration, for example, glans touching the labia. Nevertheless, that slightest penetration should be proved beyond reasonable doubt. For example, where a medical report indicates that, though the hymen was not broken, abrasions which were suspected to be the result of a slight penetration were visible. Rape can be classified as general or ordinary rape, or date rape.

In all rape cases, the most important element is lack of consent by the victim. As indicated in Section 132, consent can be obtained by:

(a) Force
Force should not be given its ordinary meaning but it should be interpreted to mean happening or done against one's will.

If force was to mean physical strength only, then rape would be a crime if only one uses physical force to obtain unlawful sexual intercourse. Therefore, the use of force can be either actual or constructive.

(I) Rape by use of actual force
This is the use of human physical strength to overpower a woman, and it is a very common type of rape. Let us consider the following illustrations:

A, a 20-year-old young man proposed love to C, but c rejected it. He decided to have sex with her by force. One day, as C went to a stream to draw water, A followed behind. He then attacked and raped C.

A saw a very beautiful lady, C, dressed in a provocative way. Since it was in the evening, he followed her and when she reached a bush, he attacked and raped her.

(ii) Rape by use of constructive force.
Constructive force is force other than actual force.
Under constructive force, there is rape by use of emotional or mental force and rape by sedation.

(ii) (a) Emotional or mental force This has to do with feelings of a person especially, sexual feelings. The perpetrator knows that once one act is done to somebody, her state of mind would not be the same. It is common in date rape. Here is an example:

A, who knew that C was a difficult girl, decided to have sex with her. He invited her for a beer at a night-club. When she was drunk and became insensible, he proposed to her and she accepted. He then took her to his flat and had sex with her. A case of reference is that of the Queenv William.

The Queen v William Camplin (1845) 1 Cox 220. William Camplin made a girl quite drunk and, while in a state of insensibility, took advantage of the situation and violated her. The defence counsel objected that there was rape committed as the intention of giving her liquor was not to render her insensible and then have sexual intercourse with her; instead, the liquor was for the purpose of exciting her. To constitute rape, there must be force and the victim should have tried to resist that force.

In delivering judgment, after a considerable discussion, William was sentenced on the fact that the girl refused to consent as long as she had the sense or power to express such want of consent. Therefore, constructive force of using liquor was considered.

To be drunk is to take enough alcohol so that it is impossible to think or speak clearly. What constitutes 'enough' depends on whether the victim is a drinker or not. Anon-drinker can even be drunk by taking little alcohol. For somebody to be considered intoxicated or dead-drunk, the intoxication should make her insensible or incapable of understanding what was being done to her, or failed to offer resistance as she was powerless.

(ii) (b) Sedation
Sedation is the act of giving somebody drugs to make her sleep. A sedative is a drug that makes somebody go to sleep.

A, was C's boyfriend. Every time A asked for sex, C refused. One day, whilst they chatted, A added a sedative to C's drink. When she slept, A had sex with her. This is another example of 'date rape.'

Also, A, as he drove his car, saw C, a very beautiful girl at the bus stop. He gave her a lift. On the way, he asked if she preferred Coca-Cola or Fanta. C chose Fanta. A then slipped a sedative in C's drink. After taking the drink, C started dozing and finally slept at the back seat. A then drove the car into a bush and had sex with her. This is an example of general rape.

The types of rape mentioned in (ii) (a) and (ii) (b) above are very difficult to prove in a court of law, though the police have managed to secure convictions in a few cases.

(b) Means of threats or intimidation of any kind
To threaten is to say that you will cause trouble or harm to somebody if you do not get what you want. To intimidate is to frighten or threaten somebody so that she will do what you want.

A threat or intimidation may be used to obtain consent from a woman. Is she consenting or she is merely submitting to the demands? What is to consent? And what is to submit?

To consent is to agree to something. To submit is to accept the authority, control or greater strength of somebody. It is also to give in.

Also, submission means willing to obey somebody whatever he or she wants you to do.

Since to consent is to agree to something, a person consenting should be deemed to have a certain degree of intelligence. And she can consent by either actions or by words of mouth. For example, a deaf and dumb person can consent by nodding her head. A person able to speak can consent by saying 'yes' or she can consent by an action. But consent should always be free and voluntary and it can be implied or expressed, but silence does not mean consent.

Hence, a sleeping woman cannot give consent (the case of Regina versus Young below).Also, an unconscious or drugged or intoxicated or dead— drunk woman, who at the time of commission of the offence did not know what was happening or failed to give resistance because she had no physical capacity to do so, is considered raped (the case of the Queen versus William Camplin above).

There is a conflict between consent and submission. Usually, it is difficult to understand the principle of consent. Whilst consent has to do with an agreement, submission is always as a result of duty to do something (e.g. a wife submitting to her husband's sexual demands) or pressure of some kind (e.g. a threat).

In marriage (according to the Penal Code), submission means consent because when people are married, they are supposed or expected to be having sex. Firstly, the legal definition of rape includes the word unlawful. Unlawful means illegal. Therefore, it is not illegal for married people to have sex. Secondly, a husband cannot commit rape upon his wife because by contract of marriage, she gives her consent to acts of sexual intercourse with her husband.

Flowing from the fact of subsisting marriage contract, she cannot retract the consent she gave at her wedding day anytime she feels like .A husband can only rape his wife if the court has, by injunction, forbidden him from interfering with her; or he has given an undertaking in court not to interfere with her; or the parties are legally divorced. These are two different legal effects. However, the law is different in USA and United Kingdom. There, a man can rape his wife and it is called marital rape.

On the other hand, people who are not married, yet want to have sex, are supposed to ask for and obtain consent of their partners since their sexual relationship, to a certain extent, is illegal.

A husband cannot commit rape and so is an impotent person, but both can be accessories. A husband can be an accessory before the fact if he abets, aids, counsels or procures the commission of rape. This is not uncommon for men who like gambling.

If B, a husband of C, owes A some money which he borrowed during gambling, but is failing to pay. A then asks B if he could be paid back in kind by allowing him to have sexual intercourse with his wife C, and B agrees. C, unaware of the arrangement, just sees A enter her bedroom, undresses and demands sex from her just for one night. When C screams, B quickly enters the bedroom to assist A by holding his wife's hands. A and B will be arrested for rape.

A persuasive leading case in such circumstances (and indeed many situations where physical force and threats or intimidations of any kind are used) is Morgan's case.

At first, the young men were not willing to have sex but Morgan persuaded them to take the invitation seriously. According to the three men, Morgan told them to expect resistance from his wife but they were not to take her resistance seriously as it would be a mere pretence on her part so that she can stimulate her sexual excitement Mrs. Morgan was awakened from sleep and carried from the room in which she was sleeping to another room that contained a double bed. She struggled and screamed, and shouted to her son to call the police, but one of the men put a hand over her mouth. Once on the double bed, the appellants had sex with her in turn, finishing with her husband. During intercourse with the other three, she was continuously being held, and this, coupled with the fear of further violence, restricted the scope of her struggles, but she repeatedly called out to her husband to tell the men to stop.

In summing-up, the trial judge indicated that by force means exactly what physical force is. It does not mean there has to be a fight or blows have to be exchanged. It means that there has to be some violence used as a result of which her will is overborne.

The judge further indicated that the prosecution has to prove that each defendant intended to have sexual intercourse with the victim without her consent. Therefore if the defendant believed that victim was consenting to him having sexual intercourse with her, then there would be no such intent in his mind and he would not be guilty of the offence. However, such a belief must honestly be held by the defendant in the first place. Meaning that, he must really believe that she consented.

And, secondly, his belief must be a reasonable one. It should be such a belief that a reasonable man would entertain if he applied his mind and thought about the matter. It is not enough for a defendant to rely upon belief, however he honestly so hold it, if it was completely based on imagination and facts and reason—which do-you mean? It does not matter that the believe that his victim gave an encouraging indication (by the victim) which could carry some weight with a reasonable man.

The judge reached such a conclusion, of explaining consent and force, when the defendants in their defence, indicated that Mrs. Morgan manifested her sexual co—operation and enjoyment in a way which could only indicate that she was consenting. They further said that any element of resistance on her part was, according to his account, no more than playacting.

Additionally, Morgan in his evidence clearly stated that his wife agreed in advance to have intercourse with the three friends whom he had brought home and, in the event, indicated her pleasure in doing so. According to him, the only protest by his wife related to the fact that one of the men who had intercourse with her was not wearing a contraceptive sheath.

Appeals were dismissed, but the court enunciated the following point of law which is of general public importance: "Whether in rape the defendant can properly be convicted notwithstanding that he in fact believed that the woman consented if such belief was not based on reasonable grounds."

In Morgan's, case the general principle of mens rea in rape cases was applied, which is, an intention to have sex with somebody knowing that she does not consent; or recklessness as to whether she has consented or not births mens rea.

There are circumstances in which submission can be construed to mean consent. For example, a wife submitting to her husband's sexual demands. These circumstances vary from case to case. Generally, the principle that consent must be free and voluntary, whether it is given expressly or impliedly, is very important. Hence, in proving that a woman consented, there should be no traces of threats or intimidations of any kind. Of reference is that of the Queen versus Olugboja.

The defendant, S.O.O., who was a Nigerian, aged 20 at the time and studying at Oxford, had sexual intercourse with J, then aged 16, at the bungalow of his co-accused L. She had been taken there with her friends K (aged 17) and L, in a car that was driven by the defendant from a disco where they all had been dancing.

L had offered the girls a lift to their home, but the defendant had driven them to the bungalow that was virtually in the opposite direction from where they lived. This was a trick to get them to the bungalow. When they got there, both girls refused to go in, and started walking away. They did not know where they were. L followed them in the car, and after some argument they got in. After a further argument K again got out, and, as she was trying to get j out, L drove off, stopped in a lane, and raped her.

L then drove back to the bungalow, picking K up on the way, and the three of them went inside. The defendant was there, lying on the sofa asleep, and saw them arrive. J was the last to come in. She was either crying. Or obviously had been. Music was put on. J declined to dance. She went to the lavatory and returned to find L, dragging K into the bedroom. The defendant switched the sitting room lights off and told J that he was going to have sex with her. She told him that L had had her in the car and asked why he couldn't leave her alone. He told her to take her trousers off and she did because she said she was frightened. She was still crying and the room was in darkness.

The defendant pushed her on the settee and had intercourse with her. It did not last long. She did not struggle; she made no resistance; she did not scream or cry for help. She did struggle when she thought after penetration the defendant was going to ejaculate inside her, and he withdrew. She put her clothes on and the other two emerged from the bedroom, where L had raped K.

The defendant and J then went into the bedroom. She told him she was going to report him to the police. He said that if she opened her big mouth he would not take her home. He later did. Once at home, J made a compliant to her mother about L but not about the defendant. She supposed that she was more upset "about the first one, "meaning L After she had made a compliant to her mother about L, she saw the police and a doctor with whom she spent a total of eight hours. She made no complaint against the defendant; indeed she said he had not touched her.

The police initially saw the defendant as a witness to the complaints by both J and K with regard to the rapes on each of them by L. In the course of the interview, the police said to the defendant that L had said that he, the defendant, had sexual intercourse with J. When they put it to him, J had made no complaint against him, the defendant at once admitted he had had sexual intercourse with J and in answer to the question: "Did she consent?" He replied: "Well not at first but I persuaded her."

At the end of the interview, the defendant made a written statement. The police then saw J who said that the defendant had indeed had a sexual intercourse with her against her will. The police then went back to see the defendant and to put to him what J had said. There followed a further long and detailed interview.

At the trial, a submission was made at the conclusion of the case for the Crown on behalf of the defendant that there was no case to answer. The judge ruled that the case should go to the jury. The defendant did not give evidence, but relied on his statement to the police as constituting his defense. The defendant was convicted to 30 months imprisonment.

The appeal of this case raised a lot of issues in regard to consent. The appellant claimed that the judge misdirected the jury as to the meaning in law of "lack of consent", and by inviting them to consider the question of consent as one of fact .The appropriate position is that where a woman in sound mind consciously permits a man to have intercourse with her, the act is only to be considered as being committed without her consent if her will was overborne by force, fear or violence or duress, or fraud. It is wrong to think that any other threat vitiates consent.

The jury considered section 1 of Chapter 82. Section 1 (of Chapter 82) of the Sexual Offences Amendment Act 1976 states as follows:

(1) For the purpose of Section 1 of the sexual offences Act 1956 (which relates to rape) a man commits rape if: a. he has unlawful sexual intercourse with a woman who a the time of the intercourse does not consent to it; and b. At the time he knows that she does not consent to the intercourse or he is reckless as to whether she consents to it; and references to rape in other enactments (including the following provisions of this Act) shall be construed.

(2) It is hereby declared that if at trial for a rape offence the jury has to consider whether a man believed that a woman was consenting to sexual intercourse, the presence or absence of reasonable grounds for such a belief is a matter to which the jury is to have regard, in conjunction with any other relevant matters, in considering whether he so believed." [Law Reports Statutes 1976 Volume 2].

The jury, therefore, was more concerned with whether J had consented or not, that is, whether the defendant knew she had not or was reckless as to whether she consented or not. This was because the defendant never disputed that he had sexual intercourse with J, but put a defense that she consented.

The defense lawyer argued that: "It is accepted that there can be rape without violence or threats of violence when a woman is penetrated whilst she is asleep, unconscious or so ill that she has no awareness at all of what is happening similar to the case of an insane woman who has no power at all to comprehend the nature of the act. But where a woman is conscious and aware of the act proposed and decides to submit, then she may only say her act was non-consensual if her submission has been brought about through violence of fear, of threats or violence.

Many submissions will be non-consensual because they are brought about by such pressures, both <u>moral or economic pressure or even blackmail that</u> <u>should be directed to concentrate on the state of</u> <u>mind of the</u> victim immediately before the act of sexual intercourse, having regard to all the relevant circumstances; in particular, the events leading up to the act and act and her reaction to them showing their impact on her mind.

Apparent acquiescence after penetration does not necessarily involve consent which must have occurred before the act takes place. In addition to the general direction about consent which we have outlined, the jury will probably be helped in such cases by being reminded that in this context, consent does comprehend the wide spectrum of states of mind to which we earlier referred, and that the dividing line in such circumstances between real consent on the one hand and mere submission on the other, may not be easy to draw. Where it is to be drawn in a given case is for the jury to decide, applying their combined good sense, experience and knowledge of human nature and modern behaviour to all the relevant facts of that case.

Looking at it in this way, we find no misdirection by the judge in this case. J was tricked into going to the bungalow in the first place. She had already been raped by L. she was crying and frightened. She saw L, dragging K into the bedroom. The defendant was determined to have sexual intercourse with her. She was kept at the bungalow against her will until she submitted. In those circumstances, the jury were fully justified in coming to the conclusion that she did not consent. The appeal is accordingly dismissed.'

If critical consideration of Olugboja's case is taken, then, what can be said about a person in authority like a prefect, a teacher, headmaster, a lecturer, a college principal, a university chancellor, a manager, etc., who threatens or intimidates a pupil or a student or a worker into sex? It is possible for such people to submit, especially if they have broken school, college, university or company regulations. And a person in authority, by abusing the authority of his office, may take advantage of such a situation and demand sex from such a girl or a lady. If she submits, then the act is none—consensual.

The Learned Judge, quoting Judge Coleridge in Reg. v. Day (9C. &P. 722, 724) said every consent involves a submission but it by no means follows that a mere submission involves consent. Meaning that every real consent has an element of submission but the reverse is not true. Real consent should be found where a woman has freedom of choice. What determine that real consent are the circumstances and facts of the case. The general questions are: If she did not find herself in such circumstances, could she have chosen to have sex with him? What harm was in the threat and how remote was it?

So, if a girl says, "Please sir, don't expel (fire) me. I will do anything for you; whatever you shall ask from me. I promise I will do." If the person in authority says: "Alright, stop crying-. Just undress and lie on the carpet so that I can have sex with you and I promise you shall not be expelled (fired)." If the girl or lady does as directed and such a man, believing she has consented, proceeds to have sex with her, he should be arrested for rape if she later complains to the police. In such circumstances, a girl or a lady has restricted freedom of choice and if she did not find herself in such circumstances, she could not have submitted. Of course she may say: "Sir, get lost! I am not cheap." But because of fear of being expelled from school or university, or that of losing a good job, she may not utter a single word to show resistance. For a pupil, she should be considered to have such an immature mind that it is difficult to disobey a person in authority.

Whether submission will always not constitute consent is a matter of consideration by the court after looking at the facts of the case. A lawyer argued that her client committed no offence. If he did, then a film producer, who persuades an actress to submit by telling her that she would lose her part in a film if she did not, commits a crime as well.

She further argued that her client never raped J by quoting unreported case involving submission in which a police constable was found without a case to answer when he was charged with rape on the basis that he had threatened the victim that he would report her for an offence unless she had intercourse with him. [Regina versus Kirby (unreported), December 19, 1961, decided by Winn J. reported in "The Times" as a news item on December 19 and 20, 1961].

On a slightly different note of understanding submission, Smith and Hogan in their book:

Criminal Law, 8th edition, a Butter worth's publication, 1996, on page 470, argue that a woman submitting to her fiancé's sexual demands because he has threatened to disengage her cannot be considered raped. They then write: "Submission may indeed be induced by a promise (and it is clearly not rape in law if he does not) but is it not a case of submission?"

Probably, Sir John Smith and Brian Hogan were analyzing the freedom of choice that a woman has in such a circumstance. And what harm is in being disengaged by man? The harm of not marrying the one she loves of course; but it should be understood that love does end. Of course, a distinction should be made between a fiancé who says, "Well, if you have sex with me then I will marry you. But if you refuse, then the door is wide open, go and forget about me," and the one who uses physical strength to hold a girl on the bed and says, "If you don't give me sex I will not marry you." In the latter situation, such a fiancé commit s rape.

In comparison to the above, a teacher who offers examination leakage to a pupil above 16 years on the condition that she offers him sex commits no rape, unless she is below 16, in which case he can be arrested for defilement. Here is the fact of age, as an under-aged lacks capacity to give consents for sex. A lecturer, who promises to offer free marks to a dull student on condition that he has sex with her, commits no rape even if he does not fulfill his promise.

b. By fear of bodily harm

Consent obtained by threatening grievous bodily harm to somebody, by use of weapons, is not consent at all. That is, in case of threats that cause harm, whether to the victim's body or to another person close to the victim, there is no consent obtained by the perpetrator. All that the accused obtained was submission and so will be guilty of rape. All the accused obtained was submission.

Cases of such a nature are 'aggravated' rape. For instance, use of knives, guns, or indeed any weapon, amounts to rape. If a woman is threatened to be killed by a person pointing a barrel of gun at her head, she would submit to his sexual demands, but that does not mean she has consented. Also, it is not necessary that a threat should be in words. Mere actions, like pointing a gun at the victim and instructing her to undress by use of signs, are enough. It does not matter even if the woman is the one who invites a man. "Please don't kill me! Just do whatever you want." If the rapist feels that her words mean consent, then he is dead wrong, for at the time she said those words she did out of fear of bodily harm. If she was at liberty and had the freedom of choice, she could not have uttered those words. Such invitation to sexual intercourse may be due to aggravated robbery.

d. By means of false representation as to the nature of the act

A representation is the act of giving information to people about something so that they can have an idea of it. It becomes a false representation when the information given is not true. In short, a false representation is a lie as to the nature of the act. That is, the victim is deceived about the process of sex.

Consent must be voluntary, hence consent obtained by false representation as to the nature of the act is no consent at all. Thus A, a karate instructor who advises C, a member who has no idea about sexual intercourse that if she prostrates herself before him and allows him to lie on top and massage her, then her bones would be strong. If C believes what is being done to her is massaging and not sexual intercourse, it would amount to obtaining consent by false representation. This is the case, especially if C had no idea about sexual intercourse.

The leading cases of consent obtained by fraud are Regina versus Flattery and the King versus Williams.

A man, who was the choirmaster of a Presbyterian church, started teaching V voice production. He later informed her that she was not singing as she should and told her to lie down on a settee. He then removed a portion of her clothing and placed upon the lower part of her body an instrument and then told her to take a deep breath after which he examined the instruction and wrote his finding in a book . He then dropped onto her and proceeded to have sexual intercourse with her. When she said; "What are you doing?" He replied; "It is quite all right, do not worry. I am going to make an air passage. This is my method of training. Your breathing is not quite right and I have to make an air passage to make it right. Your parents know all about it. It has all been arranged, before God, V, it is quite right. I will not do you any harm.

Any other lies, which have nothing to do with the nature of the act of sexual intercourse, do not constitute rape. Therefore, a man may lie to a woman that he is rich and will marry her soon and after she consents, he has not committed rape if he fails to marry her. Equally, he may lie that he is not married when in fact he is. He may even deceive somebody that he is a prince in order to obtain quick sexual consent. Promises of promotion by superiors, even if they fail to honour their promises after sex, do not amount to rape.

Equally, a promise of employment in exchange for sex does not amount to a sexual offence even though such an employer can be arrested for corrupt practices. Also, failure to pay a prostitute after sex or giving her fake money does not amount to rape because she had been deceived. Additionally, consent is not absent where a woman knowingly submits to sexual intercourse with a man who, by fraud, has made her believe that such an act will bring about benefits or good result to her. Hence, it is not rape for a traditional doctor to have sexual intercourse with a woman as remedy for her barrenness. Even when she does not get pregnant, she cannot claim o have been raped because the traditional medicine man cheated her. Therefore a lie does not make one liable for rape, no matter how the woman was deceived.

(e) In case of a married woman by personating her husband

A person, who with intent to have sexual intercourse with a married woman by personating her husband, does so unlawfully and will be deemed to have raped her.

A had been admiring C, a wife of his friend X. And knowing that his friend, X, uses a spare key that he hides under a rock, goes to X's house, leaving X at a pub. Swiftly he enters X's house and shouts: "Honey I am back." C, who is halfway asleep, believing it is her husband X answers back and tells him to jump into bed. If A manages to have sex with C, and after sex, she discovers that it was not X she submitted to, A will have raped C. A good precedent is that of Regina versus Young, in which it was ruled that a sleeping woman couldn't consent.

Held: The victim did not consent to sex. If a man has or attempts to have sexual intercourse with a woman while she is asleep, it is no defense that she did consent as she did not resist.

Furthermore, if C and E are identical twins married to Z and A respectively. And it happens that C goes to visit E and upon arrival, E tells C that her husband, A, has gone on a business trip. Before too long, E goes for a funeral for two nights leaving C at home and instructing her to occupy their bedroom.

If, unfortunately, A returns at night when E is at the funeral, uses his spare key to gain entry into the house and believing his wife, E, is sleeping, joins her in bed. During sexual intercourse, C is alarmed as she never expected her husband, Z, to move magically from their house and join her in bed. A, had no intention to have sex with C, everything happened by mistake.

Section 10 of the Penal Code states that:

A person who does or omits to do an act under an honest and reasonable, but mistaken belief in the existence of any state of things is not criminally responsible for the act or omission to any greater extent than if the real state of things had been such as he believed to exist. The operation of this rule may be excluded by the express or implied provisions of the law relating to the subject.

Consent of a person of unsound mind

Consent of retarded persons, such as idiots and imbeciles, is no consent at all. And, for that, Section 139, relating defilement of idiots or imbecile applies. The offence in Section 139 is a felony punishable if found guilty up to the maximum of 14 years imprisonment. Reference cases are that of Fletcher and Pressy below.

Suspect was convicted of rape of a girl of unsound mind. The victim was of weak intellect, and was incapable of distinguishing right from wrong. Her mother, in her evidence, stated that the victim was not allowed to go out by herself, and that she was unable to distinguish the house in which she lived from that of her neighbours. She could not have therefore given sexual consent to Fletcher.

Suspect was convicted of rape of a lady of unsound mind. The victim told the court that on the material day, pulled up her clothes and put his 'thing' into her. She knew what he did to her was wrong—as her mother told her—but did not stop him as she did not like to hurt anybody. She did not say anything to him, as she liked to be kind to every person. This is regardless of the fact that she was hurt and her clothes were bloodstained. All this happened in the bush as she collected sticks.

Another was a married man, a grandfather and used to keep sheep as a shepherd. He knew the victim's parents and went ahead to apologize for his misdeeds. The victim was, as the mother said, proved to be an idiot.

Attempted rape

Attempted rape suffices in circumstances where the accused almost had intercourse with the complainant. In proving attempted rape, the prosecution must show that the man's mensrea was coupled with him ignoring any resistance of a woman.

If C goes to the hospital for an injection and A, a male nurse, tells her to remove her trousers and underwear, and lean forward on a bed so that he can give her an injection properly. When C does as directed, A quickly unzips his trousers and, removes his erect 'gun' and almost fires at her. But before he does so, C senses that A is about to penetrate her, screams for help. A has attempted to rape C and his liable to imprisonment for life, if found guilty. If the evidence to prove attempted rape is not sufficient, A can be found guilty of indecent assault on females.

The accused was employed by the complainant as a Attempted rape kitchen boy, he attempted to have carnal knowledge of the complainant. He went to the complainant and stated that he would wish to leave her service and demanded for wages.

The complainant was standing in the back porch of the house and told the accused to call back in the morning for his wages. The accused then leaped at her throat and pushed her to the floor of the lounge. He then sat on her thighs, put his hand on her clothes over her private part and said, "Give it to me." The complainant saw the accused unbutton his trousers, but did not actually see his penis. The accused then tried to pull up the dress of the complainant, but as he was sitting on her clothes, he was unable to do so. All this time the (Complainant) witness was struggling with the accused and pleading with him to let her go and she would pay him. The accused got up and left her alone.

Held: The witness admitted that the accused got up on his own accord; it was not through the witness' hitting him or anything like that. In order to convict on the charge of attempted rape, the prosecution must show that the accused did not only intend to satisfy his passions, but that he intended to do so at all costs and notwithstanding any resistance on the part of the woman. That was not so in this case. It is not attempted rape as the accused, on meeting resistance, voluntarily desists.

Can a female be indicted for rape?

The law says a female is incapable of committing rape. But this does not mean she cannot be indicted for rape as a principal offender.

All the parties partook of the whisky, and it appeared that Mrs. Ram forced the girl to drink. The male prisoner then went upstairs to bed. Shortly after, the female prisoner forcibly took the girl up to the man's bedroom, where he had sexual intercourse with her.

The defense lawyer took objection that a woman is incapable of rape. Therefore she cannot be indicted for rape jointly with her husband. Clearly, she cannot be indicted separately.

The prosecutor argued that the indictment was for a felony. Any two or more persons can be jointly charged with a felony as principal offenders or accessories before the fact.

The judge declined to quash the indictment for rape against the female prisoner.

Date Rape

Date rape is a term given to rape that takes place between persons that know each other. It does not matter whether they know each other well or whether they are close friends or not. In effecting an arrest, an accused person cannot be charged with 'date rape' for there is no such offence enshrined independently in the Penal Code.

There is only rape. Date rape, even though found in the English dictionary, is therefore a community term. Equally, ordinary or general rape, which refers to rape by a person not known to the victim, is also a community term. This also applies to 'aggravated' rape where a perpetrator uses a weapon.

A lot of beliefs, which can either be recognized as being traditional or western, have been attached to date rape. Due to such beliefs, the following women are likely to be victims of date rape.

I. Women who like accepting large sum of money from men, whether they are very good friends or not. The belief is, accepting abnormal amounts of money—that is money beyond her small needs—is a sign of a woman inviting a man to have sex with her.

At least, some people believe, there will be pay back in the form of sexual intercourse one day.

ii. Women who like demanding money and material things from boyfriends. Having a boyfriend does not mean the financial needs of a woman should be burdened on him. Mostly, women demand money to do hair, cosmetics, pocket money, at times even school fees, etc. When a man pounces on a girlfriend on whom he has spent so much money; she may consider how much he has spent on her. And, if she says, "no," the man would say "after all the good things I have done for you" or, "are you going to be 'eating' my money without me gaining?"

When a man admires a woman and proposes to her, it means she is clean and attractive. For her to be clean, parents or guardians will have made her look like that, if not, other boyfriends. If parents do, then they will continue maintaining her even when she has a boyfriend, until she gets married, and she won't make demands from him. If other men do, then the current boyfriend will have to give her money since, obviously, she will make demands.

It should be realized that a woman is not a calf to milk a man the way a calf does a cow. Women should learn to live within the means of their guardians or parents, and wait to finish studies, and be able to earn their own money or, get married and have authority to demand money from their husbands. Otherwise, their conscience may not allow them to say 'no' to men if they have been demanding and receiving money. Some men take advantage of such women by giving them a lot of money and later have sex with them.

iii. Women who like drinking with male counterparts or women who like taking alcohol at parties. It is not impossible for a male friend to add a sedative to a woman's beer or can make her drunk to an extent of insensibility so that it is easy for him to have sex with her.

iv. Women who like frequenting men's houses. The belief is, if a woman is frequenting a man's place, then she is asking for sex. And if a man is not having sex with such a girlfriend, then it is either he cares less about her or he is dysfunctional or impotent.

Some men say: 'A woman can't tell you that she wants sex, so if she frequents and voluntarily comes to your bedroom, she is asking for it.'

v. Desperation for marriage. A desperate woman may not say 'no' if her boyfriend pounces on her for sex. She may think 'if I say no, he may leave me.' Submitting to sex because of desperation is not rape.

Police officers always advise women and girls that acquaintances and very close friends commit date rape. To avoid date rape, a woman needs to be careful as to who she goes out to drink beer with and who escorts her at night. When she visits, she should either be in the company of someone, a close friend or a young person. If she does not trust a man, and opts to go alone to his apartment or house, she must leave if she sees him making advances towards her. It is also better to go for unopened drinks as a sedative may be added to open ones.

Revocation Of Consent

Whether consent that has been given can be revoked or not is a debatable matter. However, it is express knowledge that a woman can revoke c o n s e n t b e f o r e c o m m e n c e m e n t o f s e x u a l intercourse. So if C tells A that she is no longer in a mood for sex, A would be deemed to have raped C if he forces himself on her.

Equally, consent can be revoked when A's 'penis' is touching C's labia, before he pushes it into her body. Hence, in chapter one, where MM defiled T, it was right for him to stop because T had revoked her consent, even though consent in defilement is immaterial. But if T was 16 or over, MM could still have raped her and he cannot claim that T consented as her earlier consent was revoked. An example of revocation of consent is that of Kaitamaki versus the Queen.

In summing-up this part of the case, the trial judge said to the jury: 'I tell you, as a matter of law. . . that if, having realized she is not willing, he continues with the act of intercourse, it then becomes rape. . .?

The accused was convicted and he appealed. The appellant's lawyer submitted that, by the criminal law of New Zealand, if a man penetrates a woman with her consent he couldn't become guilty of a rape by continuing the intercourse even if after a stage he realizes that she is no longer consenting. He relied on section 127 and 128 of the New Zealand's Crimes Act 1961.

Section 127 of the Act says sexual intercourse is complete upon penetration and section 128 defines rape as an act of a male person having sexual intercourse with a woman or girl without her consent. Accordingly, he submitted that rape is penetration without consent and once penetration is complete, the act of rape is concluded. So, if a man penetrates with a woman's consent, intercourse is not rape, if it continues, because for the purpose of the Act, intercourse is complete on penetration.

This submission raised a question as to the true construction of section 127 and 128. The court of appeal by majority rejected the submission expressing the opinion that Section 127 was to remove any doubt as to the minimum conduct needed to prove the fact of sexual intercourse.

'Complete' is used in statutory definition in the sense of having come into existence, but not in the sense of having come to an end. Sexual intercourse is a continuing act which only ends with withdrawal, because the offence of rape as defined in section 128 is the act of having intercourse without consent. The appeal was dismissed.

In Zambia, there is no such provision of the law even though the courts have interpreted the offence saying 'even a slightest penetration constitutes rape.' This statement is not different from saying 'sexual intercourse is complete on penetration.' So revocation of consent is a principle that can also be a c c e p t e d i n Z a m b i a, b u t u n d e r w h a t circumstances? Indeed, it is different to measure consent. If consent is revoked, at what point can the prosecution, in order to prove rape, determine that it was properly revoked? If a man has ejaculated, this provides the police with good evidence, but is it enough for a girl to say, "I told him to stop but he continued until ejaculation."? Suppose the accused says, "Yes she told me but it was at the point of ejaculation I withdrew and some 'semen 'spilt on her thighs. I don't think I raped her'. Indeed, revocation is a debatable matter, but should a woman revoke consent, she should behave as though she never gave consent at all. She should physically start resisting further intercourse and scream at him to stop.

However the agony is when a person revoking consent is a married woman. Even if the reason for revoking consent is genuine, she can fail to report to the police. This is so, as she is scared that once her husband hears that she voluntarily consents to have sex with another man, she would be labeled a prostitute and get divorced. Hence, if the agreement before sex is that A shall use a condom as C is only helping since her husband E is studying abroad, and in the middle of sexual intercourse, the condom ruptures, and when C notices she tells A to stop, but he fails to listen to her until ejaculation, it is difficult for her to report him to the police because she revokes consent.

As a result, many women involved in adultery, who agreed with their secret lovers that a condom should be used, have regretted the act. Some have been impregnated, while others have been given the deadly HIV disease. This leaves children as destitute since there is possibility that both parents will die. Women should know that sexual intercourse by use of condom is still sex. That is why a man wearing a condom can still rape a woman.

In one famous case, one of the rapists was not using contraceptive sheath, this made the victim to cry and complain to her husband. This did not increase his sentence but reduced the sentence for the other two who wore condoms. Therefore, 'your honour, even though I raped her, I was wearing a condom,' is not a valid defence in Zambia. So, even the idea of removing a condom during sex has no effect on the law. Each woman, once she consents, must be aware of the potential risk of either contracting sexually transmitted diseases (HIV inclusive) or becoming pregnant.

The effect of any revocation of consent before any penetration is that the accused cannot be prosecuted if he did as directed by the woman. To determine whether consent that was properly given can be revoked or not depends on the circumstances surrounding the revocation. For example, if a married woman hears her husband coming whilst she is in the middle of sexual intercourse with another man, can the court consider her to have positively revoked consent? Her revocation was based on fear of being punished by her husband; if he had not come, she could not have screamed at him to stop.

Equally if a girl is busy having sex in her father's sitting room, and she hears to her demand. Hence, upon penetration, a man may stop after consent is revoked; yet the court finds him not guilty of rape. Basically, the reasonable test rule should apply: how many men in the community to which the accused belongs can behave the same way the accused did? So, how many in Zambia, if they have already penetrated, would withdraw if a woman says so?

Consent after Sex

Consent cannot be given after sex. All a woman can do is to forgive a man. Therefore, a man cannot say that she consented after he had sex with her.

Silence Does Not Mean Consent

A person who submits under a threat may remain silent and allow the perpetrator to complete the commission of a crime. The circumstances, under which a woman may submit and remain silent, differ. If A threatens C with a gun, there is a possibility that she may not even open her mouth. So, if a woman is threatened or intimidated into sex and remains silent throughout the act, it does not mean she consented. The principle of 'silence does not amount to consent' should have applied in another case, since he broke into the victim's house and probably threatened the woman into sex.

However, a person should use minimum force to prevent the commission of rape in non-aggravated situations. Therefore, if A, a friend of C, attacked C without a weapon, when she visited him, it is just reasonable that C uses minimum force to prevent A from raping her. She can struggle to free herself and or scream. To scream is to give a loud high cry, because you are hurt, frightened, threatened, etc. A deaf and dumb person cannot scream. A scream will always attract neighbours whether the rape is to take place in a house or in the office. If it is in the street at night, a passer-by may hear, and if it is in the bush, somebody may still hear. In any case, why go alone in the bush or be alone at night in the street?

When it comes to prosecuting a case, circumstances under which the victim was raped are very important. Rape has to do with lack of consent and resistance of the victim might prove the non—consent. Resistance is the use of force to oppose somebody. If the perpetrator uses non-violent force that a woman can oppose, it is necessary that she offers resistance. As much as a woman can use words to offer resistance, it is also necessary that she offers resistance by action. If a woman uses words to object to the act of intercourse, but her conduct shows consent to it, then she has not been raped for she never made resistance in good faith; instead, her resistance was pretended.

Resistance either by screaming or struggling, or both, in 'aggravated' rape is not necessary. However, screaming and struggling may help prosecute the offender, in other instances, where the perpetrator has not used any weapon. Therefore, though silence does not mean consent, it plays an important role in gathering evidence.

Furthermore, a number of women have rescued themselves, after screaming. Besides, corroborators need to confirm that they heard someone shout for help. It helps if shouting for help is before sex and not after sex.

The major problem in prosecuting rape cases is when the accused person does not deny the fact that he had intercourse with the complainant, but puts an argument that she consented. This is not unusual in date rape cases. Most accused persons would say: "Officer, I agree I had sex with her. But that does not mean I raped her. She consented to the act. In fact, she had been consenting. She was my girlfriend, until yesterday at 15:00 hours when I decided to end the relationship. Apparently it was after sex."

If further investigation shows that it was true the victim was consenting to sexual intercourse with the suspect and that she reported him because he ended the relationship, then it is in order not to arrest the suspect.

The difficulty arises in answering a question as to how many times a person can be raped. It is true a person can be raped as many times as she does not consent to sex. So, if C has sex frequently with her boyfriend, A, and after some time the relationship is ended, C cannot claim to be raped immediately the relationship has been ended. For her report can be taken as that of revenge. But, if C reports having been raped by A after many days when the relationship was ended, then A should be arrested.

Date rape has various defenses, such that the best way to deal with it is to avoid the commission of the crime.

This can be done if women are able to understand the concept of date rape and that some men may act like 'lions', especially if a woman has been obtaining huge sums of money and demanding expensive material things. Many men know that ladies do change their minds about relationships, so the thinking may be as she is benefitting, a man should benefit as well. Men must also know that it is not always that a perpetrator of date rape may go unpunished. There are a lot of cases that the police have dealt with and achieved convictions.

Women, especially virgins, should know that what they carry between their legs is very important. If they don't respect their virginity, nobody would. The idea of getting rides from people they don't know or those they can't trust has made many virgins to be raped. Virgins should avoid frequenting places of men, especially if the men are not trust worthy. Also, their extraordinary personality should make them avoid asking for and or receiving money and expensive things from boyfriends. Date rape is rarely reported to the police, due to circumstances in which the victim may find herself before sexual intercourse.

Synopsis

Rape is the act of having unlawful sexual intercourse with a woman or girl without her consent.

In order to prove rape, the sexual act needs to be: (a) Unlawful (i.e. not in marriage): (b) Without express or implied consent. The above elements are necessary and if one of them is absent, then there is no rape. For example, it is unlawful for any man to have sexual intercourse with a woman or girl he is not married to, but if she consents then there is no rape.

Silence does not mean consent.

Submission does not mean consent. But consent involves submission. A married woman is expected either to submit or consent to sexual intercourse with her husband. Due to the background of consented sexual intercourse in Zambia, a lot need to be done to educate an ordinary Zambian what actual consent is.

CHAPTER 4

Defilement

DEFILEMENT

The traditional way of understanding defilement

Zambians have traditional beliefs about sexual intercourse. Traditionally, Any girl who has reached puberty is eligible for sex and marriage. Men and girls, especially in rural areas, don't know about defilement. According to them, defilement is sexual intercourse with a girl, who has not reached puberty, or sexual intercourse with a virgin. Hence, a girl can only be defiled once, for her virginity symbolizes purity, and according to the English dictionary, to defile is to make something dirty, especially something that people consider important or holy. This understanding of defilement is acceptable both traditionally and biblically.

If a man has sex with a virgin who has reached puberty, who is under or over 16 years to whom he is not married, it is called violation of virginity. Violation of virginity can only attract compensation in form of damages. As such parents end up being compensated when their daughters aged 16 years or below who have sex for the first time. Mainly, reporting to the police is only done when a girl has not reached puberty or has reached puberty but looks very young. After first sexual intercourse, any subsequent sexual acts that she may involve herself in are not a concern to society. For she is considered to have been initiated to sex and can make decisions as to whether to have sex or not. As such, a girl of 13 years can have sexual intercourse as long as she has reached puberty and she loves the man who has promised her marriage. History has it has that some men married girls as young as 12 years. Unfortunately, even in the 21st Century, marriages with young girls are still taking place, especially in rural areas and shanty compounds.

Traditional beliefs have not spared young men and girls living in urban areas and cities. In fact, the residential area where one resides does not matter. Girls between 12 and 16, living in low-destiny areas, are willingly having sex with their boyfriends. This is because they believe that as long as they have reached puberty, they are mature enough to have sex. The situation is worse with those young men and girls living in shanties.

The legal definition of defilement

Defilement is a felony, just like rape. This felony, according to section 138 of the Penal Code, is explained as:

Any person who unlawfully and carnally knows any girl under the age of sixteen years is guilty of a felony and is liable to imprisonment for life.

Provided that it shall be a sufficient defense to any charge under this section if it shall be made to appear to the court before whom the charges shall be brought that the person so charged had reasonable cause to believe, and did in fact believe, that the girl was of or above the age of sixteen. (As amended by No.26 of 1933 and No. 25 of 1941)

A simple definition is that: Defilement is the act of having unlawful sexual intercourse with any girl under the age of 16 years.

In defilement cases, consent is immaterial. As discussed already in rape cases, where lack of consent proves rape, in different cases whether the victim consented expressly or impliedly, is not important. Defilement is another form of rape and it is called statutory rape, since Parliament has set an age-limit within which a girl cannot consent to sex.

The law on defilement or statutory rape considers girls less than sixteen years to be incapable of making sound decisions on sexual intercourse. Hence, the law is set to protect these girls from being sexually abused as well as to disallowing them from engaging in any unlawful sexual activities.

Marriage with a girl under 16

In the explanation of defilement, unlawfully means illegally. Therefore a man having sex with a girl below 16 years, to whom he is married, does so legally as long as such girl is 12 years and above and he is married to her according to customary law. If she is below 12, then both parents and husband, and any persons who supported such a marriage, should be arrested for defilement. This should be the case because previously, the age at which a girl cannot be defiled was fixed at 12 years. Why in the 21stcentury should Zambians sink so low and support a motion that was rejected in 1941? A good precedent of marriage with a girl under 16 years is Chinjamba's case,

Unlawful carnal knowledge of girl under sixteen years—Section 119 (1) of the Penal code—carnal knowledge of girl not unlawful if girl married.

On review: *held* (22-3-49):

It is not unlawful for a man to have carnal knowledge of a girl to whom he is lawfully married, despite the fact that the girl is under sixteen years of age. Woodman, J.: In this case, the accused was found guilty on his own plea of being an accessory after the fact to unlawful carnal knowledge of a girl under the age of sixteen years contrary to Penal Code Section 119 (1) read with Section 359. The accused's answer to the charge was "I admit I am a headman. I know I have a duty to prevent or report crime, I admit that I knew that had married a girl under sixteen years of age at my village and was having carnal knowledge of her and I did nothing to intervene or report to any authority this fact."

This did not amount to a plea of guilt if at the time when the carnal knowledge took place there was a valid **marriage** subsisting between the legal aged man and the girl in question **according to native customary law.**

The carnal knowledge must be unlawful and it is not unlawful for a man to have carnal knowledge of a girl to whom he is lawfully married. The court has drawn its attention to the true meaning of lawful marriages. A marriage with a girl less than 16 years can only be lawful when her parents or guardians give permission for her to marry and it is in accordance with traditional norms. Consent of a girl alone cannot make a marriage lawful. So if a man elopes or starts staying with a girl under the age of 16, he cannot claim to be married to her. Such a marriage is void, and a man should be arrested for defilement. Abinding precedent is that of Sibande versus the People.

Suspect v. The people (1975) ZR 101 (SC)

The accused was charged with defilement of a girl aged 12. Her father gave her date of birt. In answer to the charge he said: "I admit the charge. It was an arrangement for m a r r i a g e . S h e t o l d m e t h a t s h e wa s 1 5 years . . ."Aplea of not guilty was entered and the trials proceeded. He was found guilty and convicted. He then appealed and the Supreme Court of Zambia considered his case.

The appellant made an unsworn statement in which he said that he twice sent someone to see the girl's parents but that they refused to give him the permission to marry her; he then went himself but they still refused. He then spoke to the girl, who said she was ready to go with him, and they went off together.

When the appellant and the girl returned, they were taken to the chief where the girl was repeatedly asked about the marriage and she repeatedly said she was formally married to the appellant. It was abundantly clear from the evidence that the witnesses were investigating whether the parents had given their permission or at least had been asked for it. It was evident that consent to marry the girl had not been obtained from the girl's parents.

In dealing with the question of marriage, the magistrate said: 'In Zambia it is not generally unlawful for a man to have canal knowledge of a girl under the prescribed age if he is lawfully married to her.. Lawfully here means that both the parents and the girl have consented to the marriage. But unfortunately, unlike rape, consent of the girl alone cannot be raised as a defense to a charge of defilement. . ."

The defense lawyer submitted that the magistrate misdirected himself in holding that the parties were not married. He argued that there was no evidence as to the customary law in the area, and that the magistrate was not entitled to make a finding on the issue without expert evidence or advice of assessors. Additionally, he argued that there was nothing to show that according to customary law anything more was needed for a valid marriage than the agreement of the parties.

The judges considered a good deal of evidence to the contrary. Why were the appellant and the girl taken before the chief? And why, in the face of the girl's assertions that they were married, did the chief insist on verifying that her parents had been approached? It is relevant to observe also that there is no evidence that according to customary law, a man and a woman, in particular a man and a 15—year –old girl (or a girl under 16), can contract a valid marriage with no formality whatsoever and with nothing more than their own agreement It is clearly the law that if there had been evidence fit to be left to a jury that the parties were married according to customary law, the onus could have been on the prosecution to negate that suggestion. But it is not enough for an accused simply to say: "We are married", or even, "We are married according to customary law." He must at least say, "We are married according to customary law because we did this and this and this," and it would then be for the prosecution to show that the event alleged did not constitute a valid marriage according to customary law. Mere agreement between two parties (a man and a girl) should not be regarded as sufficient evidence to validate a marriage. In delivering judgment of the court, the Acting Chief Justice dismissed the appeal.

Marriage of a girl under sixteen years: analysis of Rex v. Chinjamba (1949)

The Rex versus Chinjamba case set a binding precedent on the Zambian judicial system as, well as other commonwealth countries. It must be realized that in as much as it is the duty of parliament to make laws which are called statutes or Acts of Parliament, it is the duty of the courts to interpret the same statutes. As such, courts also create laws. This second form of law is called case law or judicial precedents. Case law is vital in that it gives interpretation and the science of law is a whole lot of theory requiring legal analysis and meaning to statutes; it makes law to be appreciated as a science.

In Rex v. Chinjamba, Judge Woodman simply stated that: "It is not unlawful for a man to have carnal knowledge of a girl to whom he is lawfully married, despite the fact that the girl is under 16 years of age." However an important point that Woodman added to justify his decision is that as long as, "when the carnal knowledge took place there was a valid marriage subsisting between Fulai Njamba and the girl in question according to native customary law."

So, what did Judge Woodman mean by stating that for a marriage to be valid, the couple should marry according to customary law? Since Rex v. Chinjamba is a judicial precedent, it is better to analyze what a judicial precedent or case law is in order to answer this question.

Case law is law made by judges. Case law can either be binding (meaning that it must be followed on later cases) or persuasive (meaning that it is not binding on a judge or magistrate, but he may choose to follow it).

For a precedent to be binding, three factors must be considered:

a. It must be a ratio decidendi (not an obitter dicta),
b. It must be made by a higher court, and
c. The material facts in the old case must be similar to the material fact in the case being tried.

(a) Ratio decidendi: (in English, it means, the reason for the decision). It is the statement of law on which a judge based his decision. In Rex v. Chinjamba, Judge Woodman based his decision on 'unlawful'. The legal definition of defilement simply reads: Any person who unlawfully and carnally knows any girl under sixteen years commits defilement. Hence, for defilement to be established there must be:

> Sexual intercourse (carnal knowledge) and it
> includes even the slightest penetration.

(ii) That sexual act should be with a girl under 16 years

(iii) The consent of a girl, whether express (e.g. where a girl under 16 removes all her clothes and invites a man to have sex with her) or implied (e.g. where a man removes her clothes or makes her remove her clothes by force or any other means), is not important.

(iv) The sexual act must be unlawful (not in marriage).

In Rex v. Chinjamba, the court was satisfied with the first three points, but the fourth point could not be proved. The prosecution could not prove beyond reasonable doubt that the sexual intercourse was taking place outside marriage. It was on this statement of law that Woodman based his decision and stated that a man having sexual intercourse with a girl under 16 years does not commit an offence as long as there is a valid marriage subsisting between a girl and a man according to customary law

An *obitter dicta* (in English, it simply means other things which were said by a judge). These are other statements made by a judge which did not form the basis of his decision. Obitter dicta are not binding on subordinate or future judges and magistrates, even though they may be looked at in future cases without serious consideration. Because of this, obitter dicta (singular: obitter dictum) are not binding precedents.

(b) The precedent must be made by a higher court Case law demands that the binding precedent of a case only binds courts that are at the same level, or lower than, the court that made the decision. In Zambia the criminal justice courts in their rank are the Supreme Court Of Justice, the High Court and the M a g i s t r a t e Courts. The Supreme Court's decisions bind all lower courts. The High Court decisions bind all lower courts. Also, these decisions bind the High Court judges in later cases, but they do not bind the Supreme Court judges. All Magistrate Courts don't bind any court, not even themselves. Therefore, Rex v. Chinjamba does not bind the Supreme Court. It only binds the High Court and the Magistrate Courts. The reason is that it was decided by a High Court judge.

(c) The material facts of a case

The doctrine of precedent declares that cases must be decided in the same way only when their material facts are the same. For example, if a magistrate wishes to acquit a man arrested for defilement who claims he is validly married to a girl under 16 years, and the magistrate wishes to follow the rule in Rex v. Chinjamba, it is not enough to simply state that according to Rex v. Chinjamba, it is not unlawful for a man to be having sex with a girl under 16 to whom he is married. He must ensure that such a marriage was in accordance with the customary law of that particular area and/or tribe to which a man and a girl belong. Any differences in Rex v. Chinjamba and the case at hand will make him disregard the rule in Rex v. Chinjamba.As such judges and magistrates pay attention to differences in cases that are fundamentally similar, in order to thoroughly check for any differences in material facts so as to avoid illogical conclusions

It must be appreciated that a court is not always bound to follow a precedent wholesale. This is usually done by distinguishing the two cases. A case is distinguished when the magistrate or judge notices differences in material facts between the case before his court and a previous case's decision which the court is being invited to follow by the lawyer. Invitation to follow precedence may be even made prosecuting lawyers.

In Sibande v. the People (1975) above, the defence lawyer submitted that his client was validly married to a girl under 16 years. The Rex v. Chinjamba case dictates that if a marriage with a girl under 16 is to be valid, it must be according to customary law. He argued that the prosecution had not brought forward evidence as to the customary law in the area, and that without such expert evidence (e.g. a statement from a chief's advisor of that tribe), a magistrate was not entitled to conclude that according to customary law anything more was needed for a valid marriage than the agreement of the parties. This was a very good defense. However, the judges distinguished the material facts in Rex v. Chinjamba and the case before them (i.e. Sibande v. the People). They considered a good deal of evidence to the contrary. Why were the appellant (the man) and the girl taken before the chief? And, why even when the girl repeatedly said she was formally married to the man, before the chief, did the chief insist on ve r i f y i n g w h e t h e r h e r p a r e n t s h a d b e e n approached? The judges then said that if a man wishes to claim that he is married according to customary law, he must say, "we are married according to customary law because we did this and this and this," and it would then be for the prosecution to show that the events alleged did not constitute a valid marriage according to the customary law of that area (or tribe).

As such a valid marriage according to customary law is one where:

(i) The parents or guardians to an under 16 girl, give her permission to marry. Such permission should be before any sexual intercourse. Consent of a girl alone cannot make a marriage lawful. As such any form of elopement is defilement.

(ii) The parents or guardians exercised a duty of care. Parents are custodians of the girl and why giving her permission to marry, they must act in the best interest of the girl. Because parents have experience in marriage, they must be able to adequately advise the girl on marriage issues and, if possible, deny her permission to marry. (Sibande v. the People refers). If they allow her to get married, then they should be prepared to explain to her later in life, probably after five years, that by allowing her to get married, they gave her a better life since there was nothing more important that she could have done other than getting married. For example, there are girls aged between 13 and 16 years in more remote parts of Zambia who have not gone beyond grade seven, or who have stopped school before reaching grade seven or they have never even been to school. They can't read or write. The best option for them is marriage. However, if school is within their reach and fees are affordable, marriage should not be priority for these girls.

(iii) The parents or guardians did not marry the girl against her will.

Parents or guardians have no authority to abuse the rights of a girl by pushing her into marriage. Marriage is a contract and it must start with an offer to marry the girl (which is a proposal). A girl can either reject or accept that offer. If she accepts, then her acceptance should be assessed by parents or guardians who should give her permission to marry. Acceptance can only be made by a person to whom an offer is made. So, third parties like parents, cannot accept the offer of marriage on behalf of their daughter. If they do so, there is no real consent by one party (the girl). Such a contract of marriage is bad as there was no meeting of the minds by the parties involved. Examples of marrying a girl against her will are:

> ➤ parents forced a girl into a marriage, regardless of her resistance.
> ➤ a girl is persuaded into marriage by parents through sweet-talk. Usually, she is told about benefits of marriage, and the benefits awaiting her in that particular prospection marriage.

All under 16 years old girls who are about to be forced or persuaded into marriage should report their parents or guardians to the nearest police, or to their teachers or to civic organisations like the Movement for Prevention of Sexual Offences (MPSO), Young Women's Christian Association (YWCS), etc.

In defilement, consent of a girl is immaterial. Therefore, if a man wishes to marry a girl under 16 years, he must seek her parent's permission and he must marry according to customary law of the area. There are 72 tribes in Zambia. Customary marriages differ according to each tribe. Even then, the common way of customary marriage in many tribes is through a man proposing marriage to a girl. If she accepts, then she gets engaged. Thereafter dowry is charged and paid finally she is married. A few tribes like Namwangas of Northern Province and Tongas/ Ilas of Southern Province don't consider elopement as an unacceptable way of getting married. In fact marriage—by-capture among Ilas and Tongas though not common today, was a common way of getting a wife. Marriage-by—capture simply means a man identifies a girl and when an opportunity presents itself, he would capture the girl and take her to his hut. At midnight or early in the morning, he would inform his relatives or parents that he captured the daughter of Mr. Mweemba and she spent a night with him. His family would then go and apologise to Mr. Mweemba, after which formalities would be done and the girl is considered married. After being captured, a girl can resist sexual intercourse if she is tactical or strong enough. If she successfully resists sexual intercourse she is likely to refuse to marry him. Amongst the mentioned tribes, dowry is usually paid in form of cows. Thus, a marriage-by-capture was regarded as a small offence and a man paid more cows as dowry.

It should be understood that criminal law is above customary law. Therefore, if a man succeeds in penetrating the captured girl and the girl later refuses to marry him, the man should be reported for defilement if the girl is below 16 years. If she is above 16, he must be arrested for rape. However, such misdeeds are not easily reported to the police as parents charge a lot of cows for violation of virginity. On top of that these people respect customary law more than they respect criminal law.

Suppose a young girl is sweet-talked into marriage by her parents or guardians, and she abandons school but before turning 16 or within a reasonable time after turning 16, she realizes that she is no longer comfortable in that marriage and wishes to leave the man and go back to school, can she report her husband for defilement?

This sounds illogical, for how can the police arrest a man who married according to customary law? In such a case where there is a possibility of achieving a conviction, the police must test the law.

Even though parents are custodians of the girl, the law only permits them to help her in deciding whether to marry a man or not. Sweet-talking or manipulating a girl into marriage, particularly a school girl, is not acting in the best interest of the girl. The law of defilement considers a girl under 16 to be of so immature a mind as not to be capable of consenting to sexual intercourse and marriage. Therefore, the parents' role is to assist her make the right decision. If they succeed in persuading her through sweet-talk to marry a man, they take a big risk as they are likely to be arrested for procuring defilement when the girl has lost interest in the marriage. Her "husband" should also be arrested for defilement for he knew that the girl did not love him but the parents persuaded her to marry him. The girl's argument could simply be: "I was young at the time of marriage. I was aged 14. When he proposed to me I refused but my mother told me about numerous benefits of marriage, which up to now I have not seen. Being young I believed my mother would not betray me as she is duty bound to always protect my interests. Now that I am 16/1years, I have realised that I was sexually abused both by my mother and the man who married me. If the law on defilement protects girls below 16 years, then it should also protect me. I have been abused and I deserve justice otherwise the court will set a precedence that will make a lot of under 16 year-old girls go through traumatic marriages. Like me they will stop school because parents have lied to them that getting married is better than going to school. Such young minds trust parents, so they will obey them. These girls are likely to be like me—uneconomically empowered."

Parents and young men should know that there is no statutory time limitation in which a crime can be reported to the police. Therefore, those marrying under 16 years old girls through duress and trickery are likely to be arrested even after a long period of time has passed from the actual date of occurrence of the offence.

Having assessed what marriage according to customary laws is, it is better to state that Rex v. Chinjamba basically protects people who are in remote parts of the country. These are villagers who may never have heard of defilement. All they know is that when a girl reaches puberty, even at 13, she is eligible for marriage. Mostly, these people are answerable to traditional leaders. The chief and his village head men preside over all civil wrongs e.g. adultery cases. In many instances, they also preside over criminal offence, for example, theft of foodstuffs, assault, defilements, etc. Defilement in this case is treated as a civil wrong where a girl aged 15, is impregnated, her father will only be paid damages for violation of virginity. If a case has to be reported to the police, a very senior village headman or the chief himself will decide that it be so. These people are ignorant about many things. Some have never seen a car. Others have never seen a tarred road, whilst others have never stepped their feet into a classroom ever since they were born. They can't write nor read English. Section 7 of the Penal Code states that ignorance of law is not a defence to a crime unless knowledge of the law by the offender is expressly discovered to be the reason why the offender committed the offence. Even though illiteracy is a misfortune not a privilege, these illiterate villagers know nothing about the law on defilement. May be that was why Woodman acquitted the village headman. Even the way the case starts, "A villager, Fulai Njamba, married . . ."

Not all people who are in villages are protected by Chinjamba's case for there are villages which are rooted in the interior of a town. An example of such a village is Chitulika in Mpika district. The residents of such villages are from different tribes. These are villagers who have an understanding of the law because they went to school. Some of them are pensioners with educated children. The headman is just a figure-head. He is not even informed of people who commit offences and later get arrested by the police. Violation of virginity is reported straight to local courts.

All the people living in urban areas are not protected by Rex v. Chinjamba. For how can they explain that they are married according to customary law when they don't even understand their own customary law? Even if a man claims that marriage is valid as he married according to customary law, which village headman or chief's advisor will be there to support that defence? As a result, if parents in a compound, say Matero, Lilanda, Mandevu, Chaisa, Bauleni,etc. married off a girl under 16 years and they cannot explain that such a marriage is in accordance to their traditional customary law and that they did not act in the best interest of the girl, probably they even forced her to abandon school, it is better for the police to arrest them. The numerous elopements of girls under 16 years happening in these compounds don't constitute valid marriages, as such they are tantamount to defilement. If parents to these girls don't report to the police, they must be arrested for concealment of defilement under Section 113 of the Penal Code.

Abinding precedent like Rex v. Chinjamba can cease to be binding if:

a) It can be overruled by a higher court. The Supreme Court can overrule Rex v. Chinjamba as it is higher in hierarchy than the High Court which decided it. To overrule a case is to change the case law in that case, but this does not reverse the actual decision in that particular case.

(b) Parliament amends the law.
Parliament is the highest law making body of a country and its statutes automatically overrule case law. As such, Parliament can make amendments

to the definition of defilement. This can be done by removing 'unlawfully'. Thus, the definition would be:

1. "Any person who carnally knows any girl Under 16 years is guilty of a felony and is liable to life imprisonment."

2. "Any marriage with a girl under 16 is void." This will ensure full protection of girls under 16 years though a lot of villagers will be jailed for marrying girls under 16. This is because it will take a long time for them to be aware of the law. As a result, such an amendment is not necessary. The law is weak, as some people think. Firstly, it gives a maximum sentence of life imprisonment. At times, considering to the circumstances in which the offence was committed, the quality of evidence and the mitigation of the accused, the sentence reduces to a certain number of years. Secondly, the judges have decided over various cases which form judicial precedents. In Rex v. Chinjamba, the law is that if a man claims to be validly married to a girl under 16, he must satisfy the count that he is married according to customary law. In Sibande v. the People, the law is that a man cannot contract a valid marriage with a girl under 16 years without the permission of her parents and as such, elopement of an under 16 is defilement.

Currently, there is no case law that supports the idea that if parents fail to act in the best interest of the girl and marry her off blindly, they have acted unlawfully and liable for defilement. However, let's take a look at the following situation:

According to the Oxford Advanced Learners Dictionary, sexual intercourse means: "the physical activity of sex, usually describing the act of a man putting his penis <u>inside</u> a woman's vagina." Regardless of this definition, the judges turned round and said even a slightest penetration constitutes sexual intercourse. For example, the glans of a penis touching the labia even if the hymen is not broken. Here, the judges were looking at the intention of Parliament. Parliament, did not intend to give sexual intercourse its literal meaning, but its intention was to punish anyone whose sexual organ comes in contact with a woman's sexual organ in an illegal way, like rape and defilement. So, even if the word unlawful means, "Not allowed by law," the judges should not use the literal rule and give it its literal meaning, but they should look at the intention of Parliament. Looking at the intention of Parliament is applying the mischief rule of interpreting Acts of Parliament. This rule allows the court to go behind the actual wording of a statute in order to give effect to the intention of Parliament. Unlawfully means illegally and a person having sex with an under 16 to whom he is married does so legally or lawfully. Thus, the only way to make sex with a girl under 16 lawful is by her getting married. Honestly, no one can reasonably agree that by including unlawful in the definition of defilement the intention of Parliament was to allow parents make their under 16 years old daughters abandon school and get married so that men they have procured to be having sex with these girls can be doing so lawfully. And, which person would say it is lawful and reasonable for parents to pull a girl from school and offer her marriage? As such, the same judges who gave a wider meaning to sexual intercourse should do the same with the mild unlawful. Henceforth, if Parliamentarians' intention was not to allow girls abandon school for marriage, then the judges should simply state that: it is not unlawful for a man to be having sexual intercourse with a girl under 16 to whom he is married as long as he is married to her according to customary law and such a marriage was in the best interest of the girl. "Best interest" of the girl does not mean she wants to get married. It means marriage was the only remaining thing that she could have as she was not going to school. It also means she must be a girl of good health.

This will encourage and enable girls who desire to finish grade 12 to do so. It is by examining the statutes, case law and current times that judges make new case law. Case law is helpful as Parliament cannot include everything in statutes. If that be the case, statutes will be too bulky and boring to read and difficult to understand. Case law is also easy to change through overruling and distinguishing of cases. It must be appreciated that unless the police test the law by arresting and prosecuting a parent for (procuring) defilement as she married out her daughter without acting in the best interest of the girl, the judges will never come up with that law.

In the legal system, can a girl be defiled more than once?

To answer such a question, it is vital to consider an example. A, as he drove his Toyota Cressida around Kabwata area saw C. He admired her nice legs and hooted to attract her attention. When she turned, she gave him what A termed a 'killer smile'. Soon they became lovers and frequently had sex. A few months later A discovered that, C at 15, was in fact a common prostitute going to bars and night-clubs. Despite this information, he did not end the relationship. One day, A's wife got wind of the relationship and went and shouted at C's mother. When C returned from where she was having sex with A, her mother out of revenge took her to the police station. A medical report was issued and the girl was taken to University Teaching Hospital. The doctor's opinion was that, C had been having sex for some time.

A was charged and arrested for defilement. In court, his defence was that C was a prostitute therefore he never defiled her. The sentencer told the court that it was necessary to curb defilement cases in Zambia. She further said a girl could be defiled as many times as she consents to sex, as long as she is under 16 years of age and there is no reasonable cause to believe that she is above 16. If five men have sex with a girl below 16, each one of them has defiled her. She then sentenced A to seven years imprisonment with hard labour.

Who can be defiled?

Any girl below 16 years can be defiled provided she consents to the act of sexual intercourse. If she does not consent, then she is raped. Basically, this is the difference between rape and defilement: If a girl consents, she is defiled; if she does not consent then she is raped. Also, any imbecile or idiot can be defiled, regardless of her consent or age.

Equally, a girl under the age of 16 who has an illegitimate child will be considered defiled provided the father of the child was found guilty and convicted of defilement. Or that her parents are willing to have him prosecuted. So, it is just in order for the police to ask what the victim did to the first offender, whether he was prosecuted or not? If he was not prosecuted and the girl's parents are refusing to have him arrested, why are they refusing?

Did they conceal the offence and now are scared of being arrested for being accessories after the fact of defilement?

Proof of age in defilement cases

Proof of the victim's age is always necessary. Hence, there must be good evidence that at the time of the offence, the girl was under sixteen years of age. The prosecution must prove the age of the girl, beyond reasonable doubt, before the court hearing the case of defilement. For this reason, adducing evidence merely as to the apparent age of the girl is not sufficient.

Today, birth records and certificates of a girl can be produced in evidence. In the absence of such evidence, one of the parents or a guardian to the girl should tell the court what the girl's age was at the time of the offence.

After such evidence, the court also by the girl's appearance, may estimate her age. In all respect, the court must be contented with the prosecution evidence of the girl's age. Abinding precedent is that of R. versus Kalasa Mvula.

R. v. Kalasa Mvula (1935) 1 N.R.L.R84

Kalasa Mvula was accused of defiling a girl under 12 years. (By then, in Northern Rhodesia, defilement was restricted to girls under 12 years). In proving the age of the girl, her mother who did not know when she was born told the court; "K was born when we reaped the groundnut crop after the year of bad famine when Bwana Thornicroft had left Petauke"

From this, the magistrate remembered that there was famine in Petauke in 1992 and Mr Thornicroft retired from the post of Assistant Magistrate at the end of 1992. The age of K was accordingly determined to be 11 years 10 months and this was in accordance with her appearance. The accused was, therefore, put on trial and found guilty of defilement .The accused was also tried, as ordered by the judge, on defilement of an idiot, as K was a girl of unsound mind. Such evidence of proving age of a girl was welcome by then, but now that people are able to read and keep records of events, such evidence cannot be admissible in court. It should also be understood that, where the girl is very young and can be identified as such by a reasonable man, documentary evidence is not necessary. This precedent directs every law enforcement officer, in dealing with defilement of idiots, if the defiled girl is below 16 years, to charge the suspect with two offences. That is defilement of girls under 16 and defilement of idiots and imbeciles.

Can a girl below sixteen years who was once married be defiled?

Section 138 talks about defilement of girls and not married or divorced women. A girl may marry at 13, and get divorced at 15. If she consents to sex with another man after divorce, she cannot be considered defiled for with the consent of her parents she was legally married before. A married girl, regardless of age, if she willingly has sex with another man, she has not been defiled, instead she has committed adultery. And, such a man cannot be arrested for defilement because he had sex with a 14 –year-old married woman. At what age can a girl consent to sex?

Section 14(1) of the Penal Code says:

Any person under the age of eight years is not criminally responsible for any act or omission.

A child under eight years cannot commit an offence. It is presumed that such a child is incapable of knowing fully what is wrong. So, even when it comes to consenting to sex, such a child may know what sexual intercourse is, though not fully understanding it. If a child said she did not consent to sex, the charge will be rape. However, charging a person who raped a girl below eight years with rape simply because she did not consent is a waste of time as defilement is easy to prove and both offences carry similar punishments of life imprisonment.

Who can defile a girl or a retarded woman?

Any male person of 12 years and above can defile a girl. Section 14(3) of the Penal Code says:

Amale person under the age of twelve years is presumed to be incapable of having carnal knowledge. (As amended by No 20 of 1953)

In 1953, it was presumed that a boy under 12 years was incapable of attaining an erection and able to penetrate a woman. Since section 14(3) has not been amended from that time, it is still held that only a male person of 12 years and above can commit a sexual offence. Hence, if a boy under 12 years has sex with a girl, probably her age-mate, he has committed neither rape nor defilement. So if a boy aged 11 years has sex with a girl aged 8, and when taken to the law enforcement agent he says, 'Officer, yes I had sex with her by force, but you can't touch me. For sure you know that I am protected by law,' should a law enforcement officer let him go without arresting him? No! He should be arrested for indecent assault. For only a child under eight years cannot commit a criminal offence, indecent assault inclusive.

What is indecent assault?

Section 137(1): indecent assault on females says: *Any person who unlawfully and indecently assaults any woman or girl is guilty of a felony and is liable to imprisonment for 14 years. (As amended by No. 26 of 1933)*

Law, in its fairness to young boys, protects the from predatory women under section 157. Section 157:Assault on boys under 14 years, says: Any person who unlawfully and indecently assaults a boy under the age of 14 years is guilty of a felony and is liable to imprisonment for 7 years. (As amended by No. 20 of 1953)

Assault means attacking someone physically or emotionally to an extent of injuring or making him or her uncomfortable. Indecent means an acts or behaviour that is morally or sexually offensive. Indecent assault is a sexual assault on somebody, but one that does not amount to rape.

Unlawfully here means illegally. Therefore, acts permitted by law do not constitute indecent assault. Hence a person allowed by law to examine another person, for example a medical doctor, can't indecently assault a boy less than 14 years when performing his or her duties. Equally, a mother attending to her son, for example, when bathing him, has not indecently assaulted him.

Indecent assault can be committed by:

a. Unlawful and intentionally touching someone indecently. For example, touching of the breasts, buttocks, sexual organs, etc.

b. Intentional mental or emotional assault without touching somebody. For example, a naked woman or man moving towards another person with an intention of assaulting him or her.

In point (a) above, the circumstances leading to indecency are immaterial and neither is it necessary to prove that the victim was aware of the assault. In Zambia, traditionally, some tribes are allowed to play cousinship. For instance, the Bembas play cousinship with Ngonis. If the way they play constitutes indecent assault, for example, touching of the woman's private parts by her male workmate, and the woman complains to the police, it is not necessary to prove that the woman expected or was aware of the act, since she was a tribal cousin.

In point (b) above, it is taken for granted that recklessness of a person alone is not enough to prove that he or she committed indecent assault. For the offence to be committed, any reasonable person should be sure that he or she is witnessing an indecent assault. For example, if a woman lies naked on her back and invites a 13 year old boy to have intercourse with her, the boy is simply witnessing an act of indecency and should report the woman to the police, for her act of indecency has caused an emotional attack that made him feel uncomfortable.

Mere recklessness or accidental indecency, which has no element of intention, cannot constitute indecent assault. Hence, a girl aged 16 who accidentally saw a manhood of a man who was urinating in the bush, cannot claim to have been indecently assaulted.

In order to prove indecent assault, the prosecution has to prove that:

a. T h e a c c u s e d i n t e n t i o n a l l y i n d e c e n t l y assaulted the victim,

b. The assault is one that would be considered as indecent assault by any reasonable person, and c. The girl assaulted, even if she consented to acts of indecency, was below 12 years of age and, if it is a boy, he was below the age of 14 years. If it is a woman, it must be proved that she did not consent to acts of indecency.

Does Section 157 protect a boy of 14 and below from defiling a girl? No, it doesn't. The age of the victim and perpetrator are very important. If a 12 ½ years old boy has sex with a nine-year-old girl with her consent, then he defiled her. If on the other hand, the same boy has sex with a 16-year-old girl, with her consent, then she has indecently assaulted him. If, however, he has sex with a girl aged 16 without her consent, then he has raped her and he should be treated as a rapist. The trial court before which such a matter is presented may order that the boy be counseled instead of sentencing him.

A boy above 14 years old, say one who is 15, is capable of defiling a girl if she consents. It does not matter whether the girl is of his age or older than him. Usually, such cases are rarely reported to the police, as many times, the parents feel too shy to do so, thinking society will end up mocking them since their daughter is older than the boy. If reported, the police would deal with the case appropriately. However, since a girl can be defiled as many times as possible, if a man older than her obtains sexual consent from her, then parents are quick at reporting him to the police.

Like in rape, consent of a girl of and above 12 years; and that of a boy of and above 14 years is a defence. In forthcoming amendment of the Penal Code, the age at which a girl cannot consent to act of indecency is likely to go up, probably up to age 16. This is because the last amendment to Sections 137 and 157 were made in 1933 and 1953 respectively, and when increasing the age of defilement from 12 to 16 years in 1941, indecent assault on girls and women was not reviewed.

What are the possible causes of defilement? The causes of defilement can be categorized as: I. Ignorance of law concerning defilement

Many persons lack knowledge on defilement. For young men, they go to an extent of claiming that the girl is their girlfriend. Some men arrested for defilement have claimed that they did not know that having sex with a girl below 16 years is an offence. 'How can you arrest me for having sex with my girlfriend?' shouted one young man.

Section 7 says:

Ignorance of the law does not afford any excuse for any act or omission which would otherwise constitute an offence unless knowledge of the law by the offender is expressly declared to be an element of the offence.

In accordance with Section 7, ignorance of law cannot be used as a defence in the court of law. "Your honour, I didn't know that having sex with an imbecile or idiot is an offence" cannot sustain a charge of defilement.

ii. Lack of knowledge of the law by girls
Many girls under 16 years do not know that the law protects them against sexual abuse. As such, they should not entertain any form of sexual intercourse.

iii. Peer pressure among girls
Some, and indeed the majority of girls, may even know that legally they are protected, as well as that the law sounds a warning to them that legally they are considered incapable of making a sound decision towards sexual

intercourse, yet some peer pressure may push them into this premature sexual intercourse.

Unfortunately, girls say, 'everybody is doing it'. Jane has a boyfriend and she is having sex, why shouldn't I?' 'The law on defilement was last amended in 1941 when the girls were old fashioned, so if you can't have sex, you will be a 1941 girl

Many under 16 year old girls hide sexual relationship from guardians and parents, a situation that has made some men to take chances, hoping to escape liability after sex.

iii. Lack of respect for virginity
Society has lost respect for virginity, making many girls to have sex in the early days of their youth. If virginity is respected, girls will keep it for a longer time.

(v) Selfish love by men
A man may know the law of defilement but he won't bother to explain it to a girl. The better thing a man can do if he is in love with an under 16, is to show his interest at a distance so that she knows his intentions and wait until she turns 16, to propose to her.

However for some men, instead of their friendship ending only in, 'I was missing you? How have you been my friend?' They go a step ahead and propose and later on have sex with an under sixteen. 'If I can't have sex with her now, when will I do it?' So they say, thereby falling into the crime of defilement. i. Eagerness and impatience. Anxiety about what sex is, resulting in a few girls demanding for it sometimes, a girl may be under 16, but has a boy to 'die' for. When he proposed to, she may consider herself lucky and accept the proposal. Some are unfortunate and they end up being abused. Here is an example.

A was 23 when he proposed to C, a 15-year-old girl. They agreed that they would not have sex until C was 16. Before C became 16, she enticed A into sex. One day she went to A's room at college. She was in a miniskirt. When A complained, she pulled the skirt up and taunted him that if he won't have sex with her then he was impotent. A, aggrieved by C's 'insults' had sex with her and she lost her virginity. After two months, her parents discovered that she was pregnant and her mother reported A for defilement. After considering the facts of the case, the sentencer gave Aa lenient sentence.

A girl assisting a man to defile her

A girl may expressly assist a man to defile her. The question is whether the law relating to principal offenders should be applied on her as an aider, abettor, procurer or counselor.

A, a 25-year-old man, who had never had sex before was proposed to by E, a 15-year-old girl, who had sexual experience with her former boy friend. A few weeks later, E went to A's house and enticed him to have sex with her. A, knowing that he didn't know how to have sex, explained his unfounded fears to E. E assured him that all would be all right as long as he obeyed her instructions. She then helped him remove his clothes and later on removed hers, and lay on the bed. A managed to have sex with E. The fourth time they had sex was in E's bedroom and E's mother, C, saw them busy having sex.

A was later taken to the police station where he gave a voluntary statement explaining how the relationship started. He expected the law enforcement officer to let him loose, but to his amazement; the 'cruel officer', as he described him, charged and arrested him for defilement. A was shocked, as he knew to defile is to make dirty something that is pure, and E was not a virgin. In fact she initiated him into having sex.

Traditionally, a girl like E is supposed to be scorned. But legally, the law protects E. Defilement has nothing to do with consent by a girl. It has to do with age. Therefore, a girl who consents the way E did is still a defiled girl. So the best that a man can do, when a girl is stripped off and invites him, is to run away.

In sentencing a defiler like A, the sentencer shall not consider the role played by the victim in assisting the offender in either starting or completing the commission of the crime. For, when a law is set for the protection of a certain class of people, no such person of that particular class who is a victim can be guilty of the offence committed as result of the role she played as an aider, abettor, procurer or counsellor. Lord Coleridge propounded this principal in the case of the Queen versus Tyrrell.

The Queen v. Tyrrell (1894) 1 QB 710

The defendant, J.T., was in 1893, tried and convicted on the first count of having aided and abetted, counseled, and procured the commission of unlawful sexual intercourse (in Zambia it could have been defilement) of her by Thomas Ford whilst she was between the ages of 13 and 16.

On the second count, she was charged, tried and convicted for having falsely, wickedly and unlawfully solicited and incited Thomas Ford to commit the same offence on her. At trial, it was proved that, J.T. did in fact aid, abet, solicit, and incite Thomas Ford to commit the offences on her.

The question for the opinion of the court was, whether it is an offence for a girl between the age of 13 and 16 to aid and abet a male person in commission of an offence with her, or to solicit and incite a male person to commit her offence on her.

It is impossible that the legislature, in enacting the offence of unlawful sexual intercourse on girls aged between 13 and 16, could have intended that girls for whose protection it was passed should be liable to prosecution under it.Agirl under sixteen is treated as if so immature a mind as not to be capable of consenting. The defilement assumes that she has no *mens rea,* and so cannot, therefore, be treated as capable of aiding and abetting.

Lord Coleridge, Chief Justice, in summing-up indicated that the Criminal Law Amendment Act of 1885 was passed for the purposes of protecting girls. At the time it was passed there was a discussion as to what point should be fixed as the age of consent. The discussion ended in compromise, and the age of consent was fixed at 16. With the object of protecting girls,

Parliament has made illicit sexual intercourse with a girl under that age unlawful. If a man wishes to have licit sexual intercourse with a girl, he must wait until she is 16, otherwise he breaks the law. But it is not possible to say that the offence of unlawful sexual intercourse (defilement), which is absolutely silent about aiding, or soliciting or inciting, can have intended that the girls for whose protection it was passed should be punished under it for the offence committed upon themselves. J.T.'s conviction was quashed.

It therefore follows that, it is not a criminal offence for a girl under 16 to aid or abet a male person in committing defilement, or procure or counsel him to commit defilement on her. So, if a girl says, "Please John, let us have sex," when John knows that she is under 16, he commits an offence of defilement. In this case, all the girl has done is to consent to sex, and in defilement cases, consent is immaterial, and she cannot be indicted for defilement for having abetted or aided or counseled him to have sex with her.

Notwithstanding the above, the sentencer, in cases similar to the one above involving A as the accused, E, as a victim and C being E's mother as the complainant, will consider E's intelligence. The mental capacity of the girl should be assessed. If she is found to be a normal girl, then when sentencing A, it is just in order that the sentence exercise adequate leniency. He/she can give A a fair sentence especially a one-year community sentence at the nearest government institutions. On the other hand, if the girl is very young, say 11 years old, the accused should not expect any leniency, for he should have been the first person to admonish her and later report to her parents.

Additionally, if E's mother, C, says, "My daughter has a disease of the mind," and A also knew this fact and a psychiatrist's or psychotherapist's report substantiates C's claim, then A will have defiled an imbecile or an idiot.

Defilement cases are the easiest to prosecute.

Usually, the victim is a reluctant witness. The complainant, C, is either a guardian or a parent especially the mother. Unless there was forceful penetration as discussed in rape cases, the girl may be dragged to court as a witness. Comments like, 'Officer, even if my mother wants him arrested, I love him,' have been made in most cases.

However, if the victim procured the commission of the offence, then the accused will have a valid defense if only his act was not willed by his mind. This is because at the time of committing the offence, he was unconscious or asleep, hence his mind was not in the right state and any *actus reus* was a result of involuntary movements of his body.

For Example, if E, a 14-year-old beautiful girl, adds a drug that increases sexual ability in men to A's drink and E's action is followed by her adding a sedative again to A's drink, without his knowledge, after which A falls asleep. In the meantime, because of the first drug, he had an erection whilst asleep. And because that is what E wanted, she pulls him to her bedroom, undresses him then climbs on top of him and pushes the erect "body" into hers and starts having sex with him until, just at a point when A wakes up from his involuntary sleep, E's mother, C, enters E's bedroom and finds them having sex. A is then reported to the police and is arrested for defilement. A has a valid defence because at the time of the commission of the offence, he did not know what was happening.

Section 13: intoxication

1. Save as provides in this section, intoxication shall not constitute a defence to any criminal charge.

2. Intoxication shall be a defence to any criminal charge if, by reason thereof, the person charged at the time of act or omission complained of did not know that such act or omission was wrong or did not know what he was doing it?

a. The state of intoxication was caused without his consent by the malicious or negligent act of another person; or b. The person charged was by reason of intoxication insane, temporarily or otherwise, at the time of the act or omission.

1. Where the defense under subsection (2) is established, then in a case falling under paragraph (a) thereof the accused person shall be discharged.

2. Intoxication shall be taken into account for the purpose of determining whether the person charged had formed any intention, specific or otherwise, in the absence of which he would not be guilty of the offence.

3. For the purpose of this section, "intoxication" shall be deemed to include a state produced by narcotics or drugs.

Defense to charges of defilement

Part of Section 138 states that:

Provided that it shall be a sufficient defence to any charge under this section if it shall be made to appear to the court before whom the charge shall be brought that the person so charged had reasonable cause to believe, and did in fact believe, that the girls was of or above the age of 16.

'Reasonable cause to believe, and did in fact believe'. The law is not indicating to men that they should only have reasonable cause to believe that girl is or above 16, but to in fact believe that a girl is or above the age of 16 years.

As result, the accused should prove that he was certain that his decision to have sex with the victim was acceptable and appropriate at that particular time as the victim appeared to be 16 years or older. Or, he should prove that he believed the information that the victim gave him concerning her age was true. A good case of reference is that of the King *versus* Banks.

The King v. Banks (1916) 2 K.B. 621

The accused was convicted for defilement of a girl aged 14. At the trial, he did not deny having sexual intercourse with the girl but put a defense that he had reasonable cause to believe that the girl was or above 17 years. He also said that he had no idea that the girl was under the age 16 and that he did not think of her age at all, but that she had the appearance of a girl of 17. On appeal, his appeal was dismissed because the convict, though he had reasonable cause to believe the victim to be over 16, he did not have reasonable grounds to, in fact, believe that girl was of 16 and above.

Physical appearance is very important. Fatness or the height of a girl should not mean that a girl is 16 or above, even though a fat and tall girl with well-shaped hips and breasts may be considered to be 16. It is also important to support the reason why the accused believed the victim was 16 years or older. Hence, the school grade is important. A girl may look big but in grade five. Definitely, a grade five girl is under 16years old. May be the next question is to ask her age.

If a girl loves a man, she may lie about her age. So, if a girl says she is 16 or over, yet she looks 13, it is better to ask her grade, find out about any younger or elder brothers or sisters and their ages. So, if a girl says she is 16 and that they are not twins, it is better to end the relationship, or wait until she turns 16.

However, if an accused says before the court that he had reasonable cause to believe and in fact believed that the girl was 16 because she told him so, and the girl appears big enough to be 16 or over, then the court shall consider the accused's statement. As such, he will be acquitted. If, he claims as such, and the girl looks 12 years old, then such a claim will be disregarded.

In contrast, if a girl looks big but it is found that, actually, the man knew that she was below 16 years or that the man is a neighbour of the girl or they stay in the same neighbourhood and that he had seen the girl grow, then such a man cannot use the defense of having had reasonable cause to believe that the girl was above 16. This is the case as the court may consider the fact that the accused was familiar with the victim, hence, her age was well known to him. If A has seen E, a very beautiful girl, grow or has stayed in the same neighbourhood with her for a long time and at 15, she looks as though she is 18, it is just in order that if he has sex with her, C, E's mother should report him to the police for defilement. The appearance of the daughter should not discourage her from reporting, for A had express knowledge that E was below 16.

Duty of Magistrate to explain the proviso

It is the duty of the magistrate to explain the proviso contained in Section 138 (2) of the Penal Code, otherwise any sentence passed may be quashed. A binding precedent is that of Rversus Jovan Phiri

Rv. Jovan Phiri (1954) 5 N.R.L.R324

The accused was convicted by the resident magistrate on five counts charge of defilement of a girl under sixteen years. The accused had pleaded guilty to all counts, and was sentenced to a total of three years imprisonment with hard labour. In due course, the case came before the High Court for confirmation of the sentence, where upon it was noticed that there was no entry on the record to show whether or not the proviso to section 119 (now Section 138) of the Penal Code had been explained to the accused before the plea was taken. The proviso read as follows:

"provided that it shall be a sufficient defence to any charge under this section if it shall be made to appear to the court before whom the charge shall be brought that the person so charged had reasonable cause to believe and did in fact believe that the girl was of or above the age of 16 years.

The Judge observed that the accused admitted having had sexual intercourse with a European girl claiming that she told him that she had passed puberty. It was then suggested that, in explaining the proviso to the accused, he should have asked such questions as: "Did you think or did you believe that the victim was a full-grown woman? Or, did you think that she was fully developed and old enough for the act of intercourse? And, if the reply is 'yes' then the court should record a plea of not guilty."

The proviso to the section is so much involved in the offence charged that it should have been explained to the accused before the plea was taken. This practice should be followed in similar cases except where it is palpably obvious that the child in question is considerably below the age 16.

The judge then quashed the conviction on all five counts of defilement and sentences imposed were set aside.

Following the principle In R. v Jovan Phiri, it is necessary for a magistrate to explain the proviso to the accused unless it can be noticed by any ordinary person that without doubt, the girl defiled is below 16years.An authority in Nsofu versus the People supports this explanation.

Nsofu v. The people (1973) ZR287 (SC)

The appellant was convicted on three counts charge defilement. The three girls were aged 9, 10 and 9; their parents respectively proved these ages. The evidence indicated that the three girls were playing at the house of one of them when the appellant arrived. He took each of the girls in turn into the kitchen of the house and had intercourse with her.

The appellant appealed on the grounds:

I. that the failure to explain the proviso to Section 138 resulted in the appellant being denied the opportunity to make out a defence which that proviso creates, and ii. that the evidence put forward as corroborative was not conclusive and therefore could not be corroboration *Held*: it is a rule of practice, to which reference should be made in a number of cases, that where it appears that an un-represented accused person may be intending to plead guilty to a charge of defilement the proviso to Section 138 of the Penal Code should be explained to him. For the defence under the proviso to succeed, an accused person must satisfy the court (a) that he had reasonable cause to believe that girl was of or above the age of 16 years and also (b) that he did in fact believe this. The magistrate in his judgment specifically considered this question and said: "Having seen the girls myself, I am satisfied that no one can think that any of them could be over 16years. " even, therefore, if the appellant could have satisfied the court that he did in fact believe the girls or any of them was over the age 16 years, it is clear that he could not have satisfied the court that he had reasonable cause so to believe; the defence under the proviso could not have succeeded. It was also ruled that the evidence was properly corroborated. The appeals were therefore dismissed.

Death resulting from sex

At times, sex with young girls may result in death. This could be due to forceful penetration into the girl's vagina that is underdeveloped or as a result of infecting her with a sexually transmitted disease. Can such incidents be considered to be murder? Of course it should remain undoubtedly that a man, who during rape, covers a woman's or girl's mouth and nostrils to prevent her from screaming such that unexpected to him, she suffocates and dies, commits murder.

So, if D, 13 years old, consents to sex with A, 19, and during sex her private parts get injured and she bleeds to death, A will be deemed to have caused the death of D and he should be prosecuted for rape and murder. An authority to support the above statement is that of the Queen versus Samson Manuwa.

Regina v Samson Manuwa (1952) 5 N.R.L.R. 176

The accused was charged with murder in that during sexual intercourse with a young virgin, he inflicted gross injuries on her private parts that she subsequently died. The prosecution alleged that either the accused raped or defiled the girl, and in either case death resulted. The judge emphasized that the injuries sustained by the girl on her private parts, as described in the doctor's medical evidence, were of so severe a nature that the doctor characterized them as "gross injuries". It was from that evidence that the judge established beyond reasonable doubt that the injuries resulted from violent sexual intercourse.

"Accepting that the harm was done during sexual intercourse, it is clear that great force must have been used: this may have been due in part-as the doctor suggested-to attempt to force the male organ of a grown man into the tender and underdeveloped parts of a young girl, with the result that the perineum between the vagina and the anus was turn in a gross manner."

The court established the charge of murder in that the accused showed the necessary element of malice aforethought since the prisoner caused death of the girl in the cause of committing a felony.

'Malice aforethought shall be deemed to be established by evidence proving intent to committing a felony. '(Section 180 of the then Penal Code now Section 204 (c) of the current Penal Code). The court ruled that either the girl did not consent to sex with the prisoner, thus she was raped, or the girl was under sixteen years of age and had been defiled, the question of consent then being immaterial by reason of age.

"The prisoner should have known that the deceased had not attained marriageable age but resolved to have intercourse with her, and that he carried out his purpose recklessly and with a complete disregard for pain and suffering which he was causing her in the course of inflicting injuries which were to prove fatal.

"The circumstances of the case clearly negates any possibility that the prisoner can be said to have harmed the girl 'accidentally'. The prisoner's behaviour was brutal, and in consequence of his recklessness and negligence, he caused these shocking and fatal injuries to the young girl. I have reminded myself that he is an illiterate African." The judge's verdict was manslaughter. Equally if A, a grown up man, defiles D, a girl below 16 years and gives her a sexually transmitted infection and eventually as a result of such a disease she dies, A will be deemed to have murdered D. This is because D's consent will not be considered, as she is incapable of consenting to sex. A good case to refer to is R. versus Greenwood.

R.v. Greenwood (1857)7 Cox 404

The prisoner was indicted for murder and rape of a child under ten. It appeared from the evidence that the prisoner had sexual intercourse with the deceased, and that it was afterwards discovered that she had a sexually transmitted infection.

Judge Wightman told the jury that the malice, which constitutes murder, might either be expressed or implied. There was no pretence in this case that there was any malice other than what might be implied by law.

The jury states that they were satisfied that he had sexual intercourse with her, and that her death resulted there from, but were not agreed as to find him guilty of murder. The jury instead found a verdict on manslaughter.

If it is a girl above 16 who dies as a result of a sexually transmitted infection contracted from A, A cannot be considered to have caused her death for she was capable of consenting to sex and ready to undertake any risks of sexual intercourse including pregnancies and HIV/AIDS.

Lapse of time in reporting cases to the police

There is no statutory time limitation in which a criminal offence can be reported to the police. Hence, an offence, be it rape, defilement or murder, can be reported at any time. For example, a woman who was raped 20 years ago can walk into a police station and report. "Officer, 20 years ago, I was raped by Mr. XY, the current Managing Director of XY Investments." Such a complaint is genuine but the only hindrance would be lack of good corroborative evidence. As such, when it goes for perusal to the Director of Public Prosecutions, it can be rejected.

It is indeed interesting for the police to investigate a sexual offence that occurred many years ago. But is it possible to find tangible corroborative evidence that can be used to successfully prosecute the accused without such evidence being rebutted by the defense?

The defense may argue that the complaint is malicious. If the accused is admitting that he had sex with the complainant, he may as well say she consented to it, giving reasons why he believes she consented. The defence may as well say she consented to it, giving reasons why he believes she consented. The defence may as well say that if really she had been raped, she could have reported within a reasonable time.

Parliament has not included time factor in the Penal Code in which a criminal offence can be reported because of sensitive cases like murder. D may be stabbed to death. The killer may not be found. But twenty years later, A, who was very close to D gets drunks and picks a quarrels with E. He then warns him that he would kill him the way he killed D, by stabbing him with a screwdriver. In such circumstance, there is nothing that can prevent the police from arresting A, even if no official complaint reached the police when D was found dead.

Of course any reasonable person would argue that it is very unrealistic to report a theft after a long time. Honestly, how can a person have his radio grabbed from him by a person he knows well and each time he meets him, he says:, "Good afternoon sir " until after 10 years, when he decides to report him to the police? Such a report can be considered unreasonable, but if he says his radio was stolen under duress by the thief's son, and that now his father is dead he decided to report, it is better that his report is given serious attention. Likewise, a report of rape may nor be taken seriously after many years of its occurrence. If A rapes C, and each time she meets him she greets him: "How have you been A?" Can she, after 10 years, make a complaint to the police? Such a report can sound unreasonable, isn't it? So all cases should be reported promptly to trusted friends and relations and later to the police. Even if the perpetrator has run away, a report should be made to the police.

Nonetheless, a woman can report a rape case after a long time of its occurrence if at the time of the sexual act she submitted under duress. A girl aged 13 can be kept by her uncle who keeps on threatening her that being an orphan, if she does not remove her clothes and lie on the bed, he would send her to the village. Reluctantly, the girl may continue to submit to her cruel uncle's demands. She may continue submitting until she becomes financially independent. If, say after 12 years, she feels she cannot stand the trauma of defilement and rape, she can report to the police. If before she turned sixteen, her uncle had sex with her 80 times and thereafter 45 times, he should be charged of 80 count defilement and 45 counts of rape. For she smiled and said: 'Good morning uncle,' out of fear of being sent to the village.

In a case of defilement, a girl under law is presumed to be of such an immature mind as not to be capable of giving real consent to a man. In other words, she is incapable of possessing the right state of mind towards sexual intercourse, hence her consent is irrelevant.

This being the position of the law, it is fair enough to put into consideration that such a girl may consent to sex without necessarily realizing that she has been defiled. As such, unless her parents or guardians get wind of the sexual act, she may not take the initiative of reporting the defiler to the police. This could be that when she was defiled, she did not consider what happened to her as traumatic. Or, she did consider it to be traumatic but for various reasons, failed to report the incident(s). Some men threaten to kill the girl if she reports them. This is not unusual if the defiler is a guardian or father. Also, these girls whom the law considers to be incapable of loving sexually, may claim to be in love, but only to be rejected by their lovers after getting pregnant and later face the trauma of abortion. A girl may abort at a tender age but may not feel the trauma of abortion until she turns 16. At 16 or over, the invisible blanket that the law had covered her with is unveiled, hence, according to law, she is then in the right state of mind to appreciate what sexual intercourse is. If such is the case, and the girl realizes that she was being abused and corroborative evidence to support her claim is available, then justice should not fail to prevail.

The issue of lapse of time in criminal cases is not applicable in Zambia. However, a case in which evidence cannot be traced is a bad case and it cannot be taken to court. Today, Kenyan women, who are claiming they were raped by British soldiers are demanding for compensation in a civil court. They have produced coloured children as corroborative evidence of the alleged rape cases. Notwithstanding the above, a sexual offence should be reported within a reasonable time otherwise it could be difficult to find the evidence and later on to find the suspect guilty. A good precedent on lapse of time in reporting of rape cases is that of Ndakala versus the People.

Ndakala v. The People (1974) ZR19 (SC)

The appellant was convicted of attempted rape. The evidence against him was that he seized the complainant, knocked her down and raped her. The woman was in company of another woman; her friend. After the incident both the complainant and her friend went to a club where they did not immediately make a complaint. Their evidence was that after the incident, the appellant had come along and tried to persuade them not to report the matter, and had given a number of articles to the complainant as a bribe. Later he went to the club and asked for his article back on the ground that he had not ejaculated.

Learned judge Doyle, the then Chief Justice, said: "it is extraordinary that no complaint was made until the appellant came to the club demanding these articles back. I think all three members (referring to him and the other two judges) of the court will find great difficulty in putting a reasonable and plausible explanation on this sort of behaviour. But in fact the learned magistrate did not deal with it at all. He did not ask him the question: was the behaviour of the complainant and her witness consistent with rape?"

The Chief Justice further indicated that evidence is allowed to be given of recent complaint to show consistency and it helps the prosecution's case. Early complaint indicates the situation that is direct result of another situation. The evidence was considered unsafe and the appeal was allowed, conviction quashed and sentence imposed was set aside. This was all because no prompt report that must have been weighed in the scale against the prosecution's case was available.

Community responsibility to children

Adults have a community responsibility to children. To care and protect every child from physical and sexual assault is every adult's community responsibility.

Therefore, men and women should ensure that girls below 16 are not sexually abused. They should teach them the importance of virginity. Also, it should remain undoubted that, for men, the same girl they may abuse today, may become their wife in future. For example, if a girl is abused by a man aged 21,when she is 14, by the time he is 29 he could be looking for a lady to marry and if he never abused the girl, at 22, she could be his perfect match. It is known in Zambia that, due to economic hardships, men don't marry early. Usually, a lady 5-12 years younger may be an ideal partner in marriage.

When men abuse a girl, they forget about her. When they want to marry, they cannot marry the same girl, as they will call her a prostitute. "Juliet is now a prostitute." Such a man forgets that if he did not abuse her when she was 15, she could not have slept with other men later on, instead she could have maintained her purity.

What girls need is constant encouragement and counseling from noble young men like:

"You are a beautiful girl, take care of yourself."

"You have the potential of maintaining your purity till marriage."

"You are a good girl, keep it up. Don't imitate your friends who are having sex."

"Your parents are counting on you. Don't disappoint them."

"All the neighbours have respect for you. Don't let them down."

"Keep your purity and beauty for your husband."

A young man who says such words to a young girl would be respected. Obviously, when he proposes to such a girl someday, probably after six years, she would give him a chance because she respects him. Even if the chances of him marrying her are slim, it is just good to encourage young girls to keep themselves pure. Girls should have a community responsibility of respecting what they are taught. They should know that some men could lie to them.

Concealment of defilement

Parents and guardians have a legal obligation to report any sexual offences that occur in their homes. If a daughter is defiled, parents are first supposed to report to the police so that the perpetrator is arrested. After that, they can withdraw the case if they feel pity for the man. Failure to report the defilement by either the parent or guardian is an offence referred to as compounding a felony (defilement). To compound is to make something bad become even worse by causing further harm. It also means to conceal.

On compounding a felony, Section 113 (i) of the Penal

Code states:

Any person who asks, receives, or obtains, or agrees or attempts to receive or obtain, any property or benefit of any kind for himself or any other person upon any agreement or understanding that he will compound or conceal a felony, or will abstain from, discontinue, or delay a prosecution for a felony, or will withhold any evidence thereof, is guilty of a misdemeanor: (As amended by No 5 of 1972)

a. Parents fail to report defilement for various reasons. It could be:

—obtained property. If the defiler offers money or any other property, parents are likely not to report them to the police.

—have obtained the benefit. If the parents are friends to the defiler's relatives, they may fail to report to the police hence strengthening the friendship.

b. At times, they may report defilement but because the defiler later on gives them money, they fail to supply the police with necessary documents e.g. a birth certificate. They hope that the police will get tired of waiting and discontinue the case.

If parents do what is mentioned in (a) and (b) above, they must be arrested and charged with compounding defilement. Many mothers don't take defilement seriously because they look back at their past life. The daughter may consent to sex with her boyfriend at 15 and before reporting the abuser to the police, she looks back and realizes that the only difference is that she consented to sex much earlier than her daughter. As such, if a defiler offers money, she can conceal the offence.

It is important that parents who don't report defilement cases are arrested, otherwise the law on defilement will be selective and meaningless. The community has already witnessed cases where parents have failed to report a man for impregnating their 15-year-old daughter simply because the man has offered money or he has promised the girl marriage. Such people set a bad precedence among community members. The police should be arresting such parents, otherwise members of the public will think that VSU officers are joking with the law and the people will completely disrespect the law.

Are local courts helping parents conceal defilement?

The Zambia judicial system has a provision for local courts. The Local Courts Act, which is Chapter 29 of the Laws of Zambia, regulates these courts. These courts mainly deal with civil cases according to the customary law of various tribes, but they also deal with non-serious crimes like, contempt of court. A local court justice, who in most cases has no legal knowledge but understands the customary law of his area well, heads these courts. Today, most local court justices are retired civil servants like teachers, police officers, court clerks, etc. In regard to civil cases, local courts charge compensation in form of damages. Damages are not meant to be punitive but are there to remedy the harm done. Section 5 (1) of the Act, gives directives as to the maximum sentence that a local court justice can pass. Part of section 5(1) reads:

Local courts shall be of such different grades as may be prescribed and local courts of each grade shall exercise jurisdiction only within the limits prescribed for such grade. Provided that no local court shall be given jurisdiction –

i. To order probation or imprisonment for a period exceeding two years; or

ii. *To order corporal punishment in excess of twelve strokes.*

This means that all superior offences like defilement should be referred to subordinate courts. Local courts play an important role in society as not every civil case like violation of v i r g i n i t y, a d u l t e r y, e l o p e m e n t s, m a r r i a g e dissolutions, etc can be tried by magistrate court. It should be appreciated that local court justices are empowered under the Act to charge damages for violation of virginity, elopements and pregnancies of girls. However, these justices should be reminded that they should be referring cases involving children to the nearest police station first, unless the concerned is not a child. A child under the Juvenile Act is a person below 16 years. If a justice does so, after the police have arrested the defiler, then he can charge that defiler damages. This is true as one action can result in a criminal offence as well as a civil wrong. If a justice does not refer defilement cases to the police first, he is helping the girl's parents to conceal defilement. As such, he is an accessory after the fact of defilement and the law according to section 398 may be applied on him in his personal capacity as Mr. Bwalya and not a Mr. Local Court Justice. He may be treated as an ordinary citizen who has duty to report crime. Besides, a justice should be considered a person who understands the Local Courts Act. The Act directs him to refer serious crimes to superior courts and, defilement can be referred to magistrate courts through the police.

Reasons for protecting girls less than 16 years

Parliament has set an age-limit at which a girl cannot consent to sex. With the object of protecting girls, Parliament has made illicit sexual intercourse with a girl under that age unlawful. However, parliament has not given any reasons in the Penal Code why a girl of that age should not have sex. This has made a lot of girls under 16 to have sex.

Generally, it is agreed that girls should be protected. The following reasons contained in a letter addressed to Tendai will be helpful to girls under 16.

Dear Tendai,

Greetings in the Lord Jesus Christ and hopefully you are very fine. I take the trouble of writing this letter to you because yesterday when I phoned you, you complained that auntie Sally is not treating you well. She had the right to shout at you because you angered her. You told her that it did not matter whether you had sex at 15½ years or at 16 years. Honestly, how could you talk to her like that? When she phoned and told me that you are becoming a little problem, I suggested that she took you to the hospital for virginity examination. It is good that the doctor's opinion is that you are still a virgin. I don't need to congratulate you on that, since legally, any girl below 16 years of age is expected to be a virgin. However, if the doctor said you were not a virgin, the man who defiled you could have been arrested by now. You can now see that virginity testing was purely my idea, just to make sure that no one sex with you. So, stop hating aunt, she is a very good person to live with.

Tendai, though the Penal Code indicates that it is defilement for any girl under the age of 16 to have sex with any man, Parliament at the time it raised defilement age from 12 to 16 years in 1941, did not advance any reasons why such a girl needed to be protected. Indeed, a girl at your age with well curved hips, beautiful face and pin-pointed tea—cup shaped breasts is frequently proposed to by men and within herself she feels, it is not good for Parliament to restrict me from having sex. This is the thought of many girls and most of them hide sexual relationships, because they consider themselves grown—ups. Medical doctors say they cannot prevent a girl who has reached puberty from having sexual intercourse but certainly they have given reasons why it is dangerous for a young girl, especially one below 16 years, to involve herself in premarital sex. Some of these reasons are:

1. Pregnancies
Young girls are more likely to get pregnant as they may not have better knowledge of contraceptives. A pregnancy in a young girl is associated with several problems. These problems are:

a. Pre-term labour: the chance that an under 16 girl can deliver prematurely – before end of gestation period of nine months – is high. This may subject the baby to be put in an incubator. b. Obstructed labour: the pelvis is not yet fully developed, so they may fail to deliver. This may lead to a surgical operation. An operation has its own risks, like infection after operation and at times the uterus may fail to cure properly especially if when defiled, the girl was also infected with HIV. c. Antenatal Clinic: Usually girls fail to attend antenatal clinic regularly because they are still young. Also, the stigma of mixing with grown—up women at the clinic is another contributing factor.

2. Cervical cancer
Equally, sex increases the risk of cervical cancer. This is because the exposed surface area to the virus which causes cancer of the cervix is high in younger girls.

3. Abortion
Due to the above reasons, once an under 16 gets pregnant, a favourable option could be abortion. Abortions also have their own complications like infertility, infections of the uterus, a ray proof, removal of the womb due to infection and at times death may occur

4. Sexually Transmitted Infections (STIs)
Not every girl having sex uses a condom. If that were the case, then there would have been few cases of pregnancies and abortions. Due to defilement, HIV/AIDS is on the increase among girls under the age of 16.

5. Unstable minds
Unstable minds make them have more sexual partners. These under 16 girls have immature minds; hence they cannot make good decisions on sex. They are easily seduced and are likely to have sex with whoever pleases them. This increases their chances of catching HIV/AIDS.

Tendai, apart from medical reasons, there are several religious and social reasons advanced to discourage defilement and premarital sex. Some of these reasons are:

The contract of marriage is just like a contract of employment in that the best candidate is selected. To prepare for better job, one has to study hard. In fact, parents are concerned about the economic future of children, hence, they send them to better learning institutions. In case of marriage, there is no learning centre to which parents can send their children so that they can get the relevant q u a l i f i c a t i o n s o f m a r r i a g e. T h e r e l e va n t qualification of marriage is love. But how do you get loved? Of course it is by possessing good qualities of marriage. You need to understand that you don't get loved by possessing good qualities of marriage but by marketing the good qualities of marriage that you possess to potential husbands. What are the good qualities of marriage? Good qualities of marriage vary, but the most important quality sought by many Zambian young men is that of a 'good girl'. A good girl is one who is not sexually immoral. Sexual morality ranges from being primary virgin to being a secondary virgin. A primary virgin is a young lady who has never had sexual intercourse whilst a secondary virgin is one who had sex but now is abstaining. Usually most young men develop love easily for a primary virgin as compared to secondary one, because they can quickly trust the former than the latter. Of course, you will agree with me that it is easier for a lady without a child to get married than that with a child. Some men would say: "I can't marry a lady with a child." In the same vein, some young men would say: "I can't marry a non-virgin." Virginity is like a magnet. It pulls a man towards a young lady. I know noble and educated young men who have pleaded for marriage with virgins. My sister, Tendai, you can see that keeping your primary virginity is an honourable thing to do. However, virginity alone is not an end to a better marriage; it is just a means to a good marriage. You therefore need to add to virginity other qualities like loving and caring, humility and obedience, wisdom and education (creative), and being physically attractive and decently dressed, etc. If you want to marry a king, you better train yourself to be a queen. Kings in most cases marry virgins. In the book of Esther 2:2, 17, instructions were given to find a young and very beautiful virgin for king Xerxes to marry and Esther was identified and she became the queen. Isaac, son of Abraham was a king because he was very rich. He married Rebekah, a very beautiful young virgin (Genesis 24:16). A king for you is that newly qualified medical doctor or chartered accountant who asks you for marriage after doing an HIV test. Even the test, would just be for formality so that you can gain more confidence in him. In fact, as soon as you turn 16, it is better to do HIV test since being a virgin, you have high chance of testing negative. In future, this will help you ask a man for an HIV test, for you cannot get into relationship with a man whose HIV status you don't know, no matter how educated, humble, handsome or rich he may be. Alot of ladies who shunned doing an HIV test whilst they were virgins ended up having sex with boyfriends without doing an HIV test. Remember, if you cannot plan to succeed then you are planning to fail. If you cannot plan for a good marriage then you are planning for a bad one. Safe entry into marriage requires that you do an HIV test and you must be financially independent, so study hard. You need to avoid defilement and instead keep your virginity. Firstly, a girl below 16 years residing in the Republic of Zambia is considered to be a virgin. This is because she is a government trophy and any man who seduces her – even if she is the one who takes off her clothes – commits defilement. Under 16 years means one second before a girl celebrates her 16th birthday. The plan of the government is to protect girls less than 16 years and you need to respect that plan. In fact, any girl between 12 and 16 can help government fulfill its wishes. Secondly, after attaining the age of 16, you need to understand that Zambia has a rich culture of morality. It is on record that women at one time took care of themselves very well in the area of preserving their virginity. Most of them got good marriages and lived happily. That is why divorce cases were few. Medical ethics direct doctors to respect virginity, such that they even go to an extent of testing for it. The Bible promotes virginity too. Since history repeats itself, you and many other virgins can improve the way people understand abstinence. Finally, avoid bad company. Girls like Hollywood, that neighbour of yours, are not good. Her dressing does not portray good behaviour. She may end-up spoiling you. Now that you and I have started communicating in this manner, feel free to contact me and ask any question relating to defilement, rape and incest. You need to focus your mind on good education and a good husband. A good husband will only come if you are a good girl. Greet Aunt Sally, Uncle Siame and our cousins: Mwaka and Mutale. Your loving brother, Joe.

Synopsis

Defilement is the act of having unlawful sexual intercourse with any girl under the age of 16 years with (or without) her consent. That is why defilement is called statutory rape because parliament has fixed an age limit at which a girl cannot consent to sex, expressly or impliedly.

Hence, it is still defilement for a man to have sex with a girl less than 16 years who willingly removed her clothes and invites him to have sex with her. To prove defilement: a) The girl should be below 16 years. b) The sexual intercourse should be unlawful. c) Many people misunderstand defilement. To them, a girl is eligible for sex immediately she reaches puberty. There is a lot to be done in order to educate the young girls and young men. d) Parents who conceal defilement should be arrested under section 113 of the Penal Code.

CHAPTER 5

Evidence: How do Police deal with Rape and Defilement?

5. 1 Corroborative evidence

5.2 What corroborative evidence is needed to prove that a sexual offence is committed?

5. 3 What corroborative evidence is needed to identify the man who committed the sexual offence?

5. 4 What does the principle: 'corroborative evidence needs not be conclusive' mean?

5. 5 Withdrawal of sexual offences from the police.

In Zambia, the Zambia police service is a security wing of government empowered by law to receive complaints of a criminal nature, investigate and obtain necessary evidence, arrest and take the accused to court for trial. During trial, relevant evidence and witnesses should be produced before the court. For one to be guilty, it means, the prosecution has proved that the accused committed the offence in question.

When a person believes she did not consent to sexual intercourse or has consented but is below 16 years, she should not bath and should report to the Victim Support Unit (VSU) at the nearest police station as soon as possible. At the police station, an interview will be done and medical report form issued for her to be examined by the doctors at the nearest government hospital. The victim should be accompanied by a police officer. The police officer issuing a medical report should indicate whether actual or constructive force was used. If rape was by use of actual force, and that the victim knows the suspect, the medical report should read: "raped by a known person. Actual force was used."Also, if a sedative was used and the suspect is a known person, the report should read: "raped by a known person. Constructive force was used." This will help the doctor examining the victim to give a better opinion. If say physical force was used, there is possibility of finding bruises on the opening of the vagina and, or, injuries to any part of her body due to struggling. This is the case since forceful penetration results in bruises or extensive damage.

Equally, if the victim says she did not know how the rape happened as she was put to sleep, a doctor will check for the presence of a sedative or alcohol in her blood. The major drawback is that, not all hospitals in Zambia are equipped with necessary chemicals and facilities to conduct such tests. In addition, a sedative may not be detected due to lapse of time. Also, alcohol, after some time may not be detected.

Usually, medical evidence may show that:

1   a girl's or a woman's private parts were bruised
2   there was actual penetration or there wasn't

3   the sexual act was complete, meaning that semen was found in the woman's vagina.

4   the woman had sex for the first time or she had had sex before there was a sedative or alcohol in her blood, that is, if rape was by intoxication

5   other parts on a woman's body, e.g. the head, arms, legs, thighs, etc were bruised

6   approximate time when the rape or defilement occurred After the medical examination, or as one officer takes the victim to the hospital, the other police officer should go to the scene of crime and if possible apprehend the suspect. If the doctor's report indicates that his/her findings are consistent with the allegations made and further describes the damage or injury caused to the woman, then a statement from the victim should be recorded and a docket opened. The docket, which is the case record for rape or defilement, should be given an occurrence book (OB) number. The victim is at liberty to ask for an OB number from a police officer.

Investigations, after the docket is opened, should commence immediately. Police investigate rape and defilement cases according to the information they have been given by the victim in regard to where the offence occurred, whether the suspect is a known person or not. The relationship between the suspect and the victim should also be told to them Rape and defilement are sensitive cases and once reported, they require quick and serious attention, or else the evidence may be lost. Hence, certain chronological procedures, as taught in criminal investigations may be disregarded. It is a matter of initiative so that evidence is not lost. In fact, initiative is very important when performing police duties. For example, if a mob brings a man apprehended for rape or defilement to a police station, a police officer who allows such a suspect to go because a doctor has not examined the person defiled is not being professional in performing his duties.

When investigating, the focus should be on whether the intercourse took place, and if truly the victim did not consent, or if she was below 16 years. Before a medical doctor signs a medical report, the interview should be restricted to name, age, residential address, who raped or defiled her, where and how the offence occurred, and whether the victim has bathed or not.

Corroborative evidence

Police officers have been taught that in rape cases, it is very easy for a person to bring a charge on another person, but very difficult to prove that the suspected person is actually the one who committed the offence. At times, out of revenge some women have lied that they were raped. Therefore, complainant's evidence shall not be conclusive; instead, it shall be corroborated. Without corroborative evidence, it is indeed difficult to convict the accused. This requires the analysis of the complainant's character, as well as that of the accused once he is apprehended. Serious consideration of certain questions such as listed below is vital:

1. Has C ever been involved in other immoral acts?
2. Before rape allegations, was there a sexual relationship between C and A?
3. Is C a woman who has been milking A of his money?
4. Did A use a weapon to get C's consent If not, did C truly make any resistance?
5. If she resisted, what is the proof that she did so?
    Did she shout for help? Who heard her scream?
6. How is the appearance of the scene of crime?
7. Who did C tell immediately after being raped?
8. How much time passed before C complained of rape?
9. Has A been accused of rape before? If so, who accused him?
10. When was he convicted and whom did he rape?
11. Is A a stranger to C? If not, is he an acquaintance of C?
12. Are there any people who have been seeing A with C? If so, how do they interpret the relationship between A and C?
13. On the material day and time, did any person see c and A? If so, did they appear to be strangers to each other?
14. How did her clothing appear after rape?

The above questions, if answered successfully, can bring forth witnesses who can corroborate the evidence of the accused, thereby determining whether to arrest A or not. Corroborative evidence can be either direct evidence, for example, an eye witness who saw C being raped, or circumstantial evidence. Circumstantial evidence is indirect or presumptive evidence, for example, appearance of a scene of crime, semen on the clothes or thighs of the victim, and many more examples.

Corroborative evidence is any information that statement or information should be independent from the complainant's statement, but it should not be different. And, it should show that, not only has a crime been committed, but also it was actually committed by the accused. How can this statement be qualified? If evidence is to be considered good corroborative evidence, then it should show that the offence was committed. It should also identify the person who committed the crime and at least it should remove any likelihood of false implication. It is important to explain more on how corroborative evidence can be of major help in a criminal court to the prosecution.

Corroborative Evidence To Indicate That The Offence Is Committed

Every police officer should know, that in rape or defilement cases, there must be corroborative evidence to indicate that the claims of the victim are genuine. In this regard, good independent corroborative evidence is the opinion of a medical doctor. As earlier indicated on what medical evidence should show, the doctor will indicate according to his findings whether the woman or girl had sex or not. This information once obtained is expert evidence, and it only indicates that a crime has been committed but does not indicate the person who committed it. The doctor, if physical force was used may indicate on the medical report that bruises on the vagina were visible and that semen was found inside. This evidence does not indicate whether it was A or B who forced his penis into the woman's vagina.

It only shows that the woman, indeed was raped. Obviously it is a man, but what is his name? Where does he live? How does he look? Such questions and many more, a medical report cannot answer. Therefore, a police officer should warn himself against the dependability on the medical report alone as to the identity of the accused. In fact it is a big mistake to think that a medical report would be enough to have an accused convicted of rape.

In the absence of a medical report, Learned Judge, Baron, the then Deputy Chief Justice of Zambia, in the case of robbery of Kalebu Banda versus the People (1977) ZR169 gave an example of evidence in a rape case. He said: "Thus, in a rape case, failure to obtain medical evidence when there was duty to do so means that, the court must proceed as if a doctor had testified that he had examined the victim and found no evidence that force was used, nor any evidence of intercourse."

Baron, Learned Judge, further stated that unless her submission was as the result of threats, there is no likelihood of her offering such resistance as may be necessary to symbolize lack of consent on her part. If that is the case and the accused person's defence is that a woman consented, then that evidence would be neutral.

But if she alleges that force was used to overcome her resistance, this notional evidence would be very strong in favour of the accused. Therefore, the arresting officer should warn himself on the importance of medical evidence where the woman alleges that force was used. Even if force was not used, the mere fact that a medical doctor certifies a medical report that the woman has had sex is enough to connect that the woman's allegations are true.

Corroborative evidence to identify the man who committed the offence.

This evidence should be information obtained according to the circumstances in which the offence was alleged to have been committed. To achieve this, a precise and thorough interview with the complainant in a favourable environment, for example, a quiet office where other officers cannot come in will be necessary.

The identity of the man who committed the crime is important. That is why the police should ask the victim the description of her perpetrator. The scene of crime should also be visited promptly so that any evidence available can be obtained. The questions put to a victim can help the police obtain such necessary corroborative evidence to prove in court that it was the accused who committed the offence. It must be borne in mind of a police officer that r e l y i n g o n u n c o r r o b o r a t e d e v i d e n c e i s unprofessional and is very dangerous. Equally, evidence from a third party like: "After being raped, she told me that she was raped by the accused," cannot be considered to be good corroborative evidence. If that evidence is to be accepted, the third party should explain why he/she strongly concluded or believed that indeed it was the accused who committed the offence. A good precedent is that of Ackson Zimba versus the People.

Suspect v. the People (1980) ZR 259 (SC)

The appellant was convicted of rape for having unlawful carnal knowledge of a woman without her consent. He was alleged to have seized a woman in the bush and raped her and thereafter, the woman was seen crying by an independent person. The complainant stated that during rape, she sustained scratches on her legs, and she said that the third party whom she met had asked her how she obtained those scratches. That person did not corroborate the evidence as to the scratches, nor did the medical report refer to any external injuries to the complainant at all.

The Learned Judge in delivering judgment of the court indicated that in the circumstances, there was a complete lack of corroboration in the case. The court considered whether the fact that the complainant was crying, when she was seen by an i n d e p e n d e n t w i t n e s s c o u l d a m o u n t t o corroboration as it may well be simulated. Meaning that such evidence may not be real; it may as well be pretended. The appeal was allowed, the conviction was quashed and the sentence was set aside.

In such a case, it could be that the investigating officer did not indicate on the medical report scratches on the victim's legs. Or, it could be that there were no scratches at all. If the doctor had passed his/her opinion as to the presence of the scratches, and the witness in giving evidence also mentioned them, there was no way the accused person could have been acquitted.

Notwithstanding the above, corroboration as to the identity of the accused may not be necessary if it can be shown that there can be no motive for the victim to deliberately and dishonestly make a false allegation against an accused. An example is where the accused is a man who had no connections, business or otherwise, with the victim. Why, out of so many men, would she single him out alone when she may not have seen him before?

Learned Judge, Ngulube, the then Deputy chief justice, qualified the above statement in the case of Suspect versus the People.

Suspect *v. the People (1982) ZR 77 (SC)*

The appellant was convicted of rape to two years imprisonment with hard labour. On appeal to the High Court, the sentence was enhanced to five years and he appealed to the Supreme Court. The victim was eight months pregnant and as she walked along a road near her village, a man on a bicycle came to her, forced her to the ground and beat her up, and threatened to kill her if she refused. He then had sexual intercourse with her against her will. Throughout the incident, she struggled and shouted for help. After raping her, the man beat her again for not succumbing quietly. She was bruised and covered in dirt and she was crying. She made an immediate complaint to several people. She also gave description of her assailant and of the bicycle he had. After some time, one of the persons she told about the rape saw the appellant who fitted the description given, both as to the attire and the bicycle. When he intercepted him, the appellant dropped the bicycle and ran into the bush. The next day the complainant identified the appellant when he came to the village to retrieve his uncle's bicycle. He was apprehended and handed over to the police, and later convicted.

One of the grounds of appeal was that the prosecution had not established that the crime had been committed at all. The court considered the evidence of her early complaint, her distressed condition, her very untidy appearance, and the substance of the medical evidence, which supposed that something had been inserted into her private parts.

The other and major ground of appeal was his identification as the culprit. The judges found that the learned trial magistrate had not applied his sound mind and thought to the issue regarding the question of identity of the accused. The judges saw this as misdirection.

"The principle upon which corroboration of an offence is required applies equally to the second element in the case, namely, the identity of the offender. For as much as there is a recognized danger of false complaint, the courts have consistently recognized an even greater danger, namely, the danger of false implication."

The Supreme Court had to deal with these two issues, namely: the identity of the accused and false implication. Agreeing with the State Advocate, the judges said that there could be no question of mistaken identity in this case. The incident occurred in broad daylight, and judging from the complainant's ability to give an accurate description, which enabled others to spot the appellant, the opportunity to make reliable observations must have been good. In relation to false implication, the court ruled that if in particular circumstances of the case it can be established that there can be no motive for the victim to deliberately and dishonestly make a false allegation against an accused, then the conviction should depend on the reliability of her evidence as to the identity of the culprit. This is a special and compelling ground, which would justify a conviction on uncorroborated evidence.

The court then agreed with the State Advocate and said: "In the instant case, there are no factors to suggest that any situation existed to propel the complainant to falsely single out the appellant, a man previously not even known to her. We have seen no motive for the complainant to falsely implicate the appellant and in the circumstances, we are satisfied that notwithstanding the misdirection, the conviction cannot be upset. "The appeal against the enhanced sentence was equally dismissed.

Corroborative evidence is of much importance because it is not impossible for a woman to give a false complaint. In this regard, whenever a case of rape or defilement is reported to the police, the investigating officer should warn himself of the possibility of false complaint by the victim. In order to rule out the possibility of false complaint, as earlier stated, corroborative medical evidence is important and it should be obtained within a reasonable time from the commission of the offence. Usually, a victim should be examined within 24 hours after sexual intercourse.

In the absence of medical evidence, other investigations have to be done such that even if the defense suggests that no rape occurred as expert evidence is not available, the prosecution should prove that indeed rape occurred. If medical evidence is absent and after investigations no other evidence is available to prove the occurrence of the offence, then such a case should be closed by the police for insufficient evidence.

In regard to false implication, corroborative evidence should be looked for in order to determine that the suspected person truly committed the crime. Indeed, it is rare to find the suspect in the act of sexual intercourse. As a result, an officer, following criminal investigation procedures, should find, and not create, evidence that should remove any possibility of false implication of the accused. For instance, if the victim describes her assailant but does not know him, once such a suspect is apprehended, it is vital to conduct an identification parade. This will remove any doubt as to the identity of the accused.

At times, the victim may identify a suspect but he puts up a defence of an alibi. An alibi is evidence that proves that a person was in another place at the time of the crime and could not have committed it. The best question is "Sir, where were you on such a day and at such and such a time?" Depending on the answer given and if it amounts to an alibi, it should be thoroughly investigated, by interviewing persons mentioned by the suspect. Failure to investigate an alibi is helping the accused to consolidate his defense. A good precedent is Suspect versus the People.

Suspect v. the People (1975) ZR13 (SC)

The appellant was convicted on a charge of indecent assault. The complainant who lived near a bar said the incident occurred at round 22.00 hours, however, the accused's defence was that by that five minutes before the offence was committed 21.55 hours—he was drinking with his girlfriend at a bar. He later went with his girlfriend to his house and they remained together until 03 00 hours. The arresting officer did not make an effort to investigate such a defence. The barman, who actually rescued the complainant when she shouted for help, making the appellant to run away was not interviewed if at all by 22. 30 hours he had seen the appellant. The officer never asked the barman if at all he saw the appellant's girlfriend. Equally, no one in the bar was asked if the appellant at the mentioned time was seen in the bar.

The judge said. "Quite clearly, if this evidence was true it was conclusive in favour of the appellant; yet the investigating officer appears to have made no attempts to verify or disapprove that evidence. The law is quite clear that where a defence of an alibi is set up and there is some evidence of such an alibi, it is for the prosecution to establish his alibi; the law as to the onus is precisely the same as in cases of self-defence or provocation."

In a rape, a law enforcement officer should investigate whether:

i. Corroborative (medical) evidence as to occurrence of the offence is available.
ii. The victim truly did not consent.
iii. Corroborative evidence as to the identity of the suspect is available in order to rule out false implication.

At times in trying to prove consent, the accused may as well be identified. For instance, in Butembo versus the People (1976) ZR193 (SC), the appellant claimed that he had negotiated with the woman to have sex with her and he paid K50 (Zambia Currency), meaning that the woman had consented to sexual intercourse. However, medical report indicated that she had sustained injuries on her person. Furthermore, as her assailant struggled to have sex with her, she used such reasonable and minimum force to resist the commission of rape and made the appellant sustain an injury, which she said had been inflicted by the sharp point of her umbrella. The sharp point of the umbrella had blood on it and when questioned by the police how he sustained it, the appellant admitted that it was the complainant who caused the injury on him.

This alone was enough corroborative evidence as to the identity of the accused. This evidence ruled out the possibility of false implication. The injuries that both the complainant and the accused sustained meant that consent was absent or if consent was earlier given, then it was revoked. If a woman freely and voluntarily consents to sex, why should she sustain injuries? And why inflict injuries on a man she freely and voluntarily told to go ahead and have sex with her? The judge found that there was enough corroborative evidence that the offence was committed and that the appellant committed the offence. Hence, appeal against conviction was court. Just like in case of rape non-consent of a woman should be proved, failure of which the accused would be acquitted. In the same way, if age is a relevant issue in defilement, then that age should be proved. This requires that either one of the parents or the guardian should be summoned to a court, in which the case is tried, to give evidence regarding the girl's age.

In regard to a defilement case, the focus during investigation should be on:

i.   Occurrence of the offence; obviously medical e v i d e n ce would bring about this corroborative evidence.
ii.   Corroborative evidence as to the age of the victim.
iii. Identity of the accused.

It is a must that corroborative evidence in regard to age of a girl should be produced in court. Just like in case of rape non-consent of a woman should be proved, failure of which the accused would be acquitted. In the same way, if age is a relevant issue in defilement, then that age should be proved. This requires that either one of the parents or the guardian should be summoned to a court, in which the case is tried, to give evidence regarding the girl's age.

The appellant was convicted of defilement contrary to Section 138 of the Penal Code. The particulars of the offence were that he had carnal knowledge of a girl under sixteen. The girl in question was said to be eleven years old. She gave this as her age. In evidence, the only reference she made to her age was in answer to a question by the court when she said she was born in 1961, and that her mother told her so *Held:* This is not satisfactory proof of age. There is abundant authority for the proposition that where the age of a person is an essential ingredient of a charge, that age must be strictly proved. It is not accepted simply for a victim to come to court and state her age. This can be no more than a statement as to her belief as to her age. The prosecution should have called one of her parents or brought further their best available evidence for the purpose of such proof. Appeal was allowed and a retrial by a different magistrate ordered.

Corroborative evidence needs not be conclusive

In as much as corroborative evidence is necessary, this evidence need not be conclusive in itself. This is a principle that Learned Judge, Baron, the then Deputy Chief Justice in the case of Nsofu versus the People (1973) ZR287 (SC), used to dismiss an appeal that evidence that was put forward as corroborative was not conclusive and therefore could not be corroboration.

In this case, the appellant defiled three girls aged nine, seven and nine respectively. The medical evidence indicated that each of the girl's hymen, was ruptured and that in each case the vagina was inflamed. The medical evidence further indicated that the condition was in each case consistent with the insertion into the vagina of a rough object but that that would only be done by an abnormal girl. This corroborative evidence indicated that the girls were defiled. But it never indicates the perpetrator.

The State Advocate, for the respondent, submitted t h r e e i t e m s o f e v i d e n c e, w h i c h a f f o r d e d corroboration of the evidence of the three girls, that it was the appellant who committed the offences. First, he mentioned the evidence of an aunt of Q—one of the girls who was defiled. She said her niece returned to her house at 16 00hours in the company of the other girl and they continued to play there. When cross-examined, she said she saw the appellant go to K's house (the house where the alleged defilements were committed) and about 1600hours saw him going from that house to his own house. Secondly, the State Advocate mentioned

Q's uncle's evidence. Q's uncle said that when he accused the appellant of having had sexual intercourse with the girl in the kitchen of K's house, the appellant denied the allegation and said that he was merely playing with them and had given each of them Five Ngwee. Finally, he pointed to the unsworn statement of the appellant in which he admitted he was merely playing with them. And in his favour, the court construed the word "playing" in its most innocent sense. But his denial of the commission of the offence did not mean a denial of his presence at the house at the relevant time. He then submitted that these three items of evidence all showed that he appellant had the opportunity to commit the offence. *Held:* there is ample evidence that the appellant had the opportunity to commit these offences. The evidence is that two of the three girls returned to the home of one of them (the girls) and remained there until about 19 00hours when the incident was reported. It seems clearly that the offence could not have been committed after 16:00 hours. The medical evidence indicated that the girls must have been defiled within, at most eight hours prior to the medical examinations, which took place between 23:30 and 23:40 hours that night. In other words, in the doctor's opinion, defilement could not have taken place earlier than about 15: 30hours.

It is therefore true, the appellant may not have committed the crimes even though he had an opportunity to do so. Mere opportunity to commit a crime does not amount to corroboration, but if the opportunity existed, then it should be able to bring in an element of suspicion. It is true also that it is theoretically possible that somebody else may have defiled the girls when they went to buy their scones. If, therefore, it were necessary, to show as a matter of law that the assumption that no one but the appellant had the opportunity to commit these offences was the only supposition which could reasonably be drawn from the facts, it might well be possible to argue that it has not been proved that no one else apart from the appellant had such opportunity. It is not necessary for corroborative evidence to be conclusive in itself; it needs only tend to confirm that the witness whose evidence requires to be corroborated is telling the truth when she says that the accused committed the offences. Appeal was dismissed.

From the case of Nsofu versus the People, the following matters of legal importance were brought forth:

i.   Corroboration is independent evidence when tends to confirm that the witness is telling the truth when she says that the offence was committed and that it was the accused who committed it.

ii. Corroboration must not be equated to independent proof; it is not evidence which needs to be conclusive in itself.

iii. Where the evidence of a witness requires to be corroborated, it is nonetheless the evidence of the witness on which the conviction is based; the corroborative evidence serves to satisfy the court that it is safe to rely on the evidence of the complainant or victim.

It is not easy to have an accused person convicted. That is why every accused person should be considered innocent until proved guilty in a court of law. The rule of law is that it is the duty of the prosecution (arresting officer and his/her witness) to prove the accused guilty. Hence, they need to prove beyond all reasonable doubt that the accused committed the rape. This is so, because it is he/she who alleges that must prove. And any doubt in evidence of the prosecution, is credited to the defence (accused and his witnesses). Therefore, in order for the police to gather proper evidence, there is need for the victim to make a complaint at the first reasonable opportunity.

When reporting, only the truth should be told to the police officer. That means no police officer entertains lies. If a complainant lies, during investigations the truth will always come out. This makes the officer to lose interest in a case and most probably recommend it for closure or that another officer investigates it. If a police officer, who can help the victim get justice, is lied to and in the end loses confidence in her, where else can she go? For example, there are women who tear pants and soil their clothes in the hope that the police will believe that they were viciously attacked in the bush. However during investigation, the truth could be that the scene where the rape is alleged to have taken places is a very clean carpet. This alone will make a police officer doubt if at all rape occurred. So, as people report rape or defilement cases, there should be genuineness in their statements, otherwise there is no police officer who would continue investigating after being lied to. Also, if a case is closed for insufficient evidence because the complainant gave a false story to the police, next time such a person is genuinely sexually assaulted, the police may doubt her story, and henceforth, relax in performing their duties or refer her to another police station without giving a reason why they have done so. Honestly, even at the next police station, she may not be attended to properly. No police officer should want to see innocent people jailed.

During a detailed interview with the victim, it is important that non-relations to the victim are sent out of the interview room. If the victim is not a minor, even relatives are not supposed to be there. The police officers (two in normal circumstances) should then interview the victim. Some common questions asked to gather more evidence during detailed interview, are as outlined in the example below:

1. The name of the victim
2. The day when it happened
3. The setting
4. The place where it happened
5. The time it happened
6. The people with the victim when it happened.
7. The reason why the victim is together with the penetrators.
8. How the penetrator look like
9. The background of the suspect.

The purpose of the statement collected: i. Record a word picture of an event for the information of a person who was not there. For example, the officers who may peruse a case record (docket) and the Director of Public Prosecutions (DPP) chambers.

ii. Assist in the examination of witnesses in court, mostly by the prosecutors.

iii. Enable the evidence to be checked with that which the witness previously made. Witnesses are at liberty to read through their statement before giving evidence.

iv. To justify any police action taken, Dockets are kept, for a certain period of time, for future use. Others are kept permanently at the National Archives.

It is a rule that the statement of a complainant or witness should be written in the actual words used by the person after an interview. The person making the statement should read through the statement and he/she should indicate that the statement has been read through and whatever is contained therein is correctly recorded before signing it. Usually the sentence, "read over and admitted to be correctly recorded", is written. The sample above is to help future victims of crimes to know how the interview may be conducted and how to give a statement and what is expected of them at a particular time.

In all criminal investigations, a police officer is supposed to be impartial. The police officer's duty when investigating a case is to find evidence and not to create evidence. If a police officer creates evidence, he or she is falsifying or fabricating evidence and is no better than a robber because in the end, an innocent person will be jailed and robbed of his freedom. Strong evidence warrants prosecution of the offender and weak evidence enables the offender to be acquitted. At times, arresting and charging a person may not be necessary, as evidence may not be present.

In rape cases, the most important corroborative evidence is the doctor's report. Is it consistent with the allegation? If the answer is no, then even if five people say they are witnesses, such a case of rape may be difficult to prosecute. In the end, it may be a case of indecent assault (on females).

The most difficult instance of proving rape is where the act of rape is not by physical force. Say, A obtained C's submission by making her drunk. It would be difficult to prove that C did not consent.

For Questions like:

1 How often is C with A?
2 What is the relationship, mere friendship or is it an intimate relationship?

3   Is the alcohol content in the blood traceable in the morning since it may be only in the morning that C will discover that a had intercourse with her?

4   How is A responding to allegations of rape?

I met her in the bar, proposed to her. She agreed and we went to my house. ii. She is my girlfriend and we have been having sex. I was drunk and so was she; therefore she can't say I raped her.

The idea behind rape is lack of consent and if that cannot be proved, then there is no offence. If consent is proved to have been absent, then the officer should look for corroborative evidence as earlier stated. Usually, circumstantial evidence is good corroborative evidence. Each VSU officer should be aware of the fact that the court would reach a verdict of guilty because the prosecution has established a prima facie case against the accused. As such, conviction starts with the police.

So, if an offence is committed and an officer gathers good evidence, there is no way an accused can be acquitted. This is because the court in Zambia is like a scale and all it does is to weigh, and according to the law established the evidence before it. If the defence produces good evidence to rebut that of the prosecution, then the accused is acquitted. If on the other hand the prosecuted produces good and stronger evidence, then the accused is found guilty and given an appropriate sentence.

In this regard, a police officer when investigating should think of the possible defence that the accused may put forward in court, as such he should know what to tell the court when such a defence is raised so that he/she is not embarrassed. Therefore, the police should deal with certain defences like insanity and intoxication. It is indeed true, according to law, that even if actus reus and mens rea of a crime are present, a good defence to such a crime will result in an acquittal of the accused.

Withdrawal of sexual cases from the police

It is important to note that, in sexual offences including rape and defilement, the accused person is at the mercy of the complainant. Should the complainant have mercy, the case can be withdrawn from the police at no cost at all. The law allows withdrawal of cases from the police as long as there is a reason to do so, even if the reason is vague. For example:

'Officer, we can deal with this case as a family matter.'

'Officer, the young man will marry the girl after she turns 16, so there is no need to prosecute him.'

'We are family of Christians, so we have forgiven him.'

Synopsis

Corroboration evidence is any evidence that supports the statement of the victim.

In rape cases, the evidence before the court should be: a) Corroboration evidence to indicate that sexual intercourse took place, e.g Medical evidence (report) b) Evidence to indicate that truly the victim did not consent to sex. c) Corroboration evidence as to the identity of the suspect in order to rule out possibility of false implication or identity.

In defilement, evidence before the court should be: a) Corroboration evidence to indicate that sexual intercourse occurred e.g. Medical evidence b) Corroboration evidence to indicate that the alleged defiled girl was below 16 years e.g. birth certificate. c) Evidence in regard to the identity of the accused person, usually victim identifies the accused.

CHAPTER 6

Incest and Unnatural Sexual Intercourse

Incest And Unnatural Sexual Intercourse

Incest is sexual intercourse between two people who are <u>closely related in a family</u>. <u>Whereas unnatural sexual intercourse is a sexual activity between two people, it is however a sexual activity.</u>

Traditionally and biblically, the two offences were regarded as taboo. If anyone had sex with a close relative, traditionally, the ancestral spirits which were believed to be the protectors of human life were considered defiled.

Certain required rituals to cleanse the family and the people involved were performed.

If, for instance, a father had sex with his daughter, the misdeed was kept a secret by the family. Even if the man's wife knew that her husband had sex with her daughter, there was nothing she did to denounce him. It was taboo and a sacred secret never to be talked about lest the gods heard and became annoyed.

Incest

Incest is an offence under the Penal Code and it prohibits relatives from having sexual intercourse amongst themselves.

Section 159: Incest by males

(I) *Any male person who has carnal knowledge of a female person, who is to his knowledge his granddaughter, daughter, sister or mother, is guilty of a felony and is liable to imprisonment for five years*

Provided that if it is alleged in the information or charge that the female person is under the age of twelve years, the offender shall be liable to imprisonment for life.

(ii) *It is immaterial that the carnal knowledge was with the consent of the female person.*

Section 161: Incest by females

Any female person of or above the age of sixteen years who with consent permits her grandfather, father, brother, or son to have carnal knowledge of her (Knowing him to be her grandfather, father, or son as the case maybe) is guilty of a felony and is liable to imprisonment for five years.

Test of Relationship In Incest Cases

The concept of brother and sister includes: half—brother (stepbrother) and half-sister (stepsister) respectively. It does not matter whether the relationship between the person charged with an offence and the person with whom the offence is alleged to have been committed is or is not traced through lawful wedlock.

Incest is a sexual relationship between relatives. Therefore, consanguinity has to be proved. Consanguinity is the relationship by birth in the same family. Hence, for incest to suffice, there must be a blood relationship between the parties involved. If a blood relationship cannot be traced, no matter how the facts of the case may present themselves, the offence is not committed.

In incest, there must be evidence to indicate that i. The accused had intercourse with the victim ii. The accused was by blood related to the victim

iii. At the time of sexual intercourse, the accused has express or implied knowledge that the victim was a blood relation, and he/she believed this fact.

A relationship by blood means exactly that, hence men who adopt pregnancies or those whose wives are impregnated by other men, are not related with the children born thereafter. Therefore, any sexual intercourse with the girl born, as long as rape or defilement cannot be proved, does not amount to an offence. It does not matter even if the daughter shares the same surname with her father. Equally, it is not incest for any person to have sexual intercourse with any adopted child. For example, a man may adopt a girl aged 10, and if at 18 he proposes to her and freely and voluntarily she consents to sexual intercourse, then he has not committed any offence. It does not matter even if they call each other father and daughter respectively. In the same way, a woman cannot be charged with incest for having sexual intercourse with an adopted son, if at the time of intercourse the boy was of and over 14 years. A good persuasive case is that of R. v. Carmichael.

The appellant later remarried and in 1932, he separated from his second wife because she had alleged that he was having intercourse with S. After this separation, the appellant lived with S. S gave birth to three children and the appellant admitted to be the father of those children. On several occasions, and at the time of divorcing his first wife, the appellant had acknowledged being the father of S and E.

The appellant's defence was that: i. He had been told by his first wife (S's mother) that S was begotten by another man and that he believed that statement to be true.

ii. He had told the second wife that he was not the father of S.

iii. He had acknowledged S to be his daughter both in his petition for divorce with his first wife as well as occasionally to avoid scandal. Even though he named her and she used his surname, he had not begotten her, so, she was a bastard of his wife.

Held: there were three elements in the charge, which had to be proved by the prosecution,

I. That the appellant had sexual intercourse with S,

ii. That S was his daughter, and

iii. That at the time when he had intercourse with her, the appellant knew that she was his daughter.

In cross-examination, the appellant's second wife had been asked if the appellant had ever told her that he was not the father of S, but the trial judge held that such a question was inadmissible. The fact that S's mother did in fact tell the appellant that he was not the child's father, and that the appellant believed her statement to be true would be enough to return the verdict of acquittal. The appeal was allowed and conviction quashed.

The Penal Code definition of incest in both cases does not include sexual intercourse with in-laws (that is, sister-in—law, brother-in-law, son-in-law, mother-in-law, father-in—law, and daughter-in—law), as incest. Usually, a conflict between Traditional Laws and Zambian Criminal Law does exist. For example, it is incest for a man to have sexual intercourse with his uncle's daughter on the basis of cousinship. That is, if A who is a son of D had sex with C who is a daughter of B and it happens that D and B are blood brother and sister respectively. This is because a blood relationship between A and C can be traced. However, traditionally, it is not a taboo for A to have sex with C. They can even marry if they so wish.

Like in defilement cases, consent is immaterial. The frequency of incest cases is not much, as most cases are shielded from the knowledge of society. This is because the traditional belief of incest is still prevailing among all classes of people, whether educated or not. At times, family members may discourage the victim, one who has the desire or who takes the initiative, to complain. "Do you want to bring this family to shame?" Keep quiet! What has happened has happened" they would say.

It should be remembered that in cases of incest, one of the persons involved could complain. For example, X and Y may be son and mother respectively, and they may have been having sex. If X complains that his mother forces him on top of her and manages to have sex with him, Y should be arrested for the offence. If it is Y who complains that whenever X comes home, he has sex with her, X should be arrested for the offence.

There are instances when close relatives can be having sex and none of them takes the initiative to report to the police. In fact, these are the most common situations. However when another relative complains to the police, then both of them should be charged and arrested for incest.

For example, A, the father, can be having sex with B, his daughter, with her consent. When C, A's wife and B's mother, discovers, she can complain to the police. A and B will then be arrested for incest. In cases of incest, a girl under 16 is not criminally responsible for the offence. Therefore, if B is under

16, then it is only A to be arrested. Also, by application of section 14(3) a boy under 12 years old cannot be charged with incest. Equally, by application of section 157, the law protects a boy under 14, if he has sex with a relative above 16, with her consent.

As earlier stated, an offence of incest cannot be committed unless one person involved is aware of the relationship or both of them are aware that they are related. Hence, there is a need to prove the relationship. This can be done by oral evidence, or producing copies of marriage or birth certificates, if available.

Hence, A, unaware that B is a relation, proposes to her and ignorant about their relationship, she accepts. Later on, B becomes pregnant and during negotiations for damages, A's father turns out to be B's father too. Both A and B cannot be charged with incest.

Cases of incest are rarely reported to the police for fear that the family would have two people imprisoned at one time. Since it is obvious that both of them would be arrested unless it can be shown that the male person involved was below 12 (or 14

—as the case may be) when the offence was committed, or if it is a girl, that she was less than 16 years of age.

Unnatural sexual intercourse

As earlier stated, this is another offence society has problems with. It is considered total taboo.

The Penal Code in section 155 explains unnatural offences and states that:

Any person who:

a. Has carnal knowledge of any person against the order of nature; or
b. Has carnal knowledge of an animal; or
c. Permits a male person to have carnal knowledge of him or her against the order of nature; is guilty of a felony and is liable to imprisonment for 14 years.

As far as section 155 is concerned, any form of sex that is against the order of performing sexual intercourse, is an offence. Anal-sex is sexual intercourse as of man's penis and anus. It does not matter whether it is a man's anus or woman's anus.

For the explanation of unnatural offences, section 155(a) and 155 (c) include homosexuality, lesbianism and heterosexuality.

i. Homosexuality: This is a sexual relationship between male persons. Hence sodomy or homosexual anal-sex is an offence. If male A has sex with male B, both A and B should be arrested.
ii. Lesbianism: This is a sexual relationship between females. If they have sex, in whatever form, they will be deemed to have had sex against the order of nature.
iii. Heterosexuality: This is relationship that subsists between people of the opposite sex. However, a man my refuse to penetrate the vagina and instead, penetrate the woman's anus. As such a man commits an offence.

Today, words like bisexual and gay are very common. A bisexual person is capable of having both anal and vaginal sex. There is no restriction as to which gender can be bisexual.

Section 155(b) is more concerned with animal sex, that is, sex between an animal and a person. It is called bestiality. For example, sex between a male dog and a woman or, sex between a female dog and a man. It does not matter whether penetration is anal or vaginal, or both.

Section 155 is enacted to curb the 'animal in man' by encouraging human beings to be having sex through the legally recognized way, which is heterosexual.

Sodomy may be explained as an unlawful and Intentional sexual through the anus between human beings. Whilst activity is the unlawful and intentional sexual activity as per anus and vagina between a human being and an animal. So, it is possible for the police to charge a person with unnatural offence of sodomy (or simply sodomy) or unnatural offence of bestiality (or simply bestiality).Any person, who permits or does not resist the commission of an unnatural offence, is guilty of the offence.

It is important to note that an offence cannot be committed if it is not done unlawfully. Hence a person who is coerced into committing an offence cannot be guilty of an offence. So if A is forced into having anal sex with his brother, he cannot be arrested for sodomy.

Equally, where there is no intention (no *mens rea*), an offence cannot be committed. For example, A commits no offence if he decides to have sex with his girl friend, C, from behind and by mistake fails to penetrate the right place and instead inserts his penis into C's anus.

Many people get involved into animal sex due to ignorance of law, which of course, is not a defense to any criminal charge. Here are three examples:

1. A—a very beautiful lady, was a student at a higher institution of learning. One day as she left Shop-rite (Supermarket), she was approached by B, a middle aged foreign woman. She told her that she liked her and if A wished, she could do research for her. A agreed and started doing some work for B. A few days later, B invited A to watch a videotape on animal sex. She then started explaining how she enjoys sex with her dog, Chewy. A became interested.

The next Saturday, when A went to work, B gave her US$100 on condition that she had sex with Chewy. That day, A had sex with a dog. She never enjoyed sex, so, B told her that if she screamed as a sign of enjoying sex, she would be paid US$120.Adid as instructed and, what started as research work ended up in animal sex.

At hen had sex with other dogs apart from Chewy. Later she was given US$50 for any nice looking student she took to B. However, the tenth lady refused and reported B to the police. 40 videotapes were confiscated from B and she was deported to her country of origin.

2. A, was a pretty girl studying at one of the higher institutions of learning. One day, B, a foreigner, gave her a lift. B proposed to her and she accepted. The third time they had sex, B told A that it was better his friend had sex with her. When she resisted, B assured her of marriage. To A's surprise, B's friend turned out to be a very big male dog. A managed to have sex with it and hoped to marry this guy who looked very handsome.

She loved him though she couldn't tell whether he was an American, European, Lebanese, Cuban, etc. All she knew was that he was a rich man from Western countries doing business in Zambia and that one day, she would marry him and fly out of Zambia.

One day, she went to see B but a security guard told her that the boss had left. He then gave her a parcel. A rushed to her room and opened the parcel. To her surprise, it was a videotape. When A watched the tape, it contained 12 ladies having sex with different dogs and she was one of them. At the end of the video tape, a voice said: "You and your friends were great performers. I have already sent the tapes to my associate and I am now a rich man. Any way, thanks for your cooperation."

A ended up in a counseling room, as comforting words from her elder sister and a close friend never helped.

3. A, a well built young man, after watching animal sex on internet decided to have sex with his dog. However, as he did so, he forgot to lock the door to his bedroom. His girlfriend came in and found him busy having sex with his dog. She silently left and came back with the police. She claimed he had contaminated her, as he could not have sex with a dog as well as with a woman. A was very surprised when the police arrested him for

unnatural offence of bestiality. He pleaded with the girl to withdraw the case. When the girl finally accepted to do so, the arresting officer severely warned him. He went home and killed the dog.

Most unnatural offences are not reported to the police. At times, even if reported to the police and the police arrest the perpetrators and the principal offenders, the accessories and offenders, if they are foreigners, have been deported to their countries of origin by the government.

In cases of unnatural offences, consent by either party is immaterial. However, defenses like insanity, confusion, etc., are available.

Synopsis

Incest is sexual intercourse between people who are closely related in a family Consanguinity has to be proved. Consanguinity: a) Is the relationship by birth in the same family: b) Is the relationship by blood

CHAPTER 7

The Way forward for Sexual Offences

THE WAY FORWARD FOR SEXUAL OFFENCES

The Zambian Penal Code has not been frequently amended, from the time it was adopted from the British.

Hence several weaknesses can be noticed. These weaknesses have made police officers to find a lot of difficulties in performing their duties. For example, there are certain bad conducts which are not enshrined in the Penal Code, and when a person has been sexually assaulted, police officers cannot do anything to help such a person. They are employed to enforce the law, and they cannot enforce a law that does not exist

Raising Defilement Age From 16 To 18 Years

There are speculations that Parliament would increase the defilement age from 16 to 18 years. The only justification at hand is that Zambia is a signatory to the convention on the rights of a child and that a child is defined as any person below the age of 18 years. It is expected that the amendment will protect girls further from predatory men, especially teachers in secondary schools. However, it is important to realize that all girls above 16 years under authority of someone are protected by section 132 (b) which says: It is rape for a man to obtain sexual consent from a woman or girl by all means of threats or intimidation of any kind. Section 132 (b) distinguishes consent from submission. Whilst it is agreed that real consent must be free and voluntary; that is, without any traces of threats or intimidation, apparent consent to intercourse is equated to submission. To submit is to accept the authority, control or greater strength of somebody. As such, authority can make a pupil to reluctantly consent to sexual intercourse with a teacher. If that be the case, then she is a rape victim, for her consent is not real. Real consent can only be found where someone has real freedom of choice and the test questions are:

i I f s h e d i d n o t f i n d h e r s e l f i n s u c h circumstances, could she have offered herself to him?

ii If her freedom of choice was not restricted, could she have offered herself to him?

If the purpose of raising defilement is to protect (school) girls, then the girls who need more protection are those at universities and colleges. These ladies under 25 year of age are at times intimidated into sex by some lecturers. It must be understood that these young ladies are vulnerable as the same lectures mark their continuous assessments and examinations within the university premises. For pupils, there is no continuous assessment and their examinations are likely to be marked in Lusaka. If a pupil is proposed to by a teacher and she says no, she can even ask for a transfer to another secondary school. If a university student says no, there is no where she can go. She may keep on avoiding the lecturer. If parliament wishes to protect young ladies from predatory men, it is better to increase defilement age to 25 years, so that sexual consent of a young lady under that age becomes immaterial. But could this be normal? No it couldn't, because by that age most ladies are married. In rural areas, by age 18, most young ladies are wives and mothers. Equally, in cities, it is not impossible to find girls aged 18 who are married.

Furthermore, government has not done enough to sensitize people on defilement. The traditional belief about defilement is still prevailing. Age is something people have not bothered much about. To them, defilement is sexual intercourse with a girl who has not reached puberty or intercourse with a virgin. It does not matter whether that virgin is below or above 16 years. Sex with a virgin only attracts damages. Reporting to the police is only done where a girl has not reached puberty. If people are still intellectually 'blind' about sexual intercourse with a girl below 16 years, wouldn't it be worse if the age of defilement is pushed to 18 years? If, since 1941, government has not sensitized people on defilement, what guarantee will it give Zambians that it shall sensitize them if the age of defilement is raised to 18? And how long will it take for government to sensitize all the people in Zambia? Ignorance of law is not a defence to a crime, but is it fair to sentence a young man who has intercourse with a 17 years-11-month-old young lady when he stays in a rural area and knows nothing about defilement of girls below 18 years?

For example, a Member of Parliament from a rural constituency can be seen chanting in Parliament supporting a motion to increase defilement to 18 years. But upon reaching his constituency he is told that his son was arrested for defiling his girl friend aged 17 years 11 months because he had promised her marriage but later changed his mind. He gets annoyed because this particular girl, though never married before, has a child.

He rushes to the police station to talk to the a r r e s t i n g o f f i c e r a n d t h e o f f i c e r r e p l i e s : "Honourable X Sir, a girl who has a child can be defiled as long as she is below the statutory age limit for defilement and that there is no record of her being lawfully married before." Honourable X waits for judgment day, and on that day the magistrate says: "Defilement of girls is a very serious offence and offenders must be punished. However, I will exercise some leniency by sentencing you to the statutory minimum sentence of 15 years imprisonment."

If Parliament wants to prove that girls are ignorant about defilement, they should do a random survey of girls aged between 14 and 16. Let virginity examinations be done on these girls and those found to have sex should be asked if they reported to their parents. The answer would be: "I don't think he did anything wrong. I allowed it because I loved him and I still love him."

The possible outcomes of increasing the defilement age:

a. **Concealment of defilement**

If a girl is about to turn 18, and she believes the man she is seeing is a potential husband, she will not tell anyone that she is having intercourse. The question is, if girls aged between 15 and 16, have been secretive about their sexual relationship, what shall be the case with girls aged between 16 and 18?

b. **Girls aged between 16 and 18 will be bad models**

Girls aged between 15 and 16 will be looking up to girls aged between 16 and 18 as models. What the older girls will do, the young ones are likely to do later. If older girls will disregard amendments to section 138 and continue having intercourse with their boyfriends, the young girls are likely to do the same when they become their age.

c. There will be lack of control

Now, it is possible for a girl aged 171/2 to advise her 15 year-old younger sister not to have boyfriends because she is still a child even if she has a boyfriend herself. After increasing the defilement age, the young sister will simply say: "You and I are graded as children by the law, yet you have a boyfriend. So, why should I not have boyfriend as well?"

d. Unnecessary withdrawal of cases

If now, cases are withdrawn from the police on condition that the young man would marry the girl after she turns 16 years of age, what more when defilement age is increased to 18?

e. Corruption is likely to increase

If a case is not withdrawn, there will be a higher chance of corruption. The evidence could either be willfully distorted or the evidence at court could be altered such that on technical grounds, the accused is acquitted or discharged. This is likely to be the case especially if a minimum sentence of 15 years is voted for.

f. Reporting of most cases by girls above 16 will be out of frustration. Asexual relationship with a girl aged between 16 and 18 may have been in existence before the amendment of section 138.After the amendment, the girl may plead with a man not to end the relationship and it is very difficult for them to start abstaining when already used to having sexual intercourse. However, upon ending a relationship, a girl would rush to the police and report thus: "Officers, I want you to arrest a defiler. Before I turned 18, he used to have intercourse with me. By then I was only a child; not able to think. Now that I am 18 ½, I have realized that I was being abused. There is good corroboration evidence to indicate that the used to have intercourse with me."

It must be appreciated that the intention of increasing the defilement age to 18 years is an honourable one.

However, it is better if Parliament would wait, say for five years, before the changes are effected. This would give government enough time to sensitize the people on what defilement is. If Zambia is a signatory to the Convention on the Rights of a Child, then all boys and girls below 18 years, should be given some privileges if they commit crimes, sexual offences inclusive. Privileges like community sentences. It should not automatically mean that girls below 18 should now be vulnerable to defilement. Each country has a background for defilement.

Instead of increasing the age limit for defilement, Parliament should enact a law to protect girls and women from being sexually harassed. It is out of sexual harassment in schools, colleges and places of work that reluctant consent to sexual intercourse arises. Sexual harassment includes: physical contact, bad comments about sex and victimization or intimidation into sexual intercourse.

Defilement Of Boys

It is legally argued that defilement has to do with penetration, and a boy cannot be penetrated. In layman's language, defilement is making something dirty and no longer pure especially something that people consider important and holy. Many outside the legal framework will agree that a young boy is such an important and holy person and can be made dirty or impure due to sexual intercourse. Equally, few in the legal system can argue that a boy cannot be made dirty or impure by having sexual intercourse with a woman.

For example, if a woman is HIV positive, can she fail to pass on a virus to a boy? It is possible she can, just like a man can infect the young girl. So, why can't a boy be defiled?

Also, it must be realized that the law on defilement was last amended in 1941. In 1941, there were few or no predatory women to lure boys into sexual intercourse. And there was no HIV/AIDS, hence defilement was referred to the destruction of the hymen but a boy hasn't got this symbol of purity. If it is agreed that a boy can be defiled, the problem will be how to gather the necessary corroborative evidence. If an older man penetrates a young girl, medical evidence will show. At least if she was a virgin, the hymen would be torn. There may also be evidence of (gross) injury to the vulva because of forcing the manhood of a grown up man into underdeveloped vagina of a young girl. The seed may also be found.

To the contrary, if an old woman has intercourse with a young boy, there will be no evidence to indicate that sexual act. This is because a woman is used to having intercourse with older men and a young boy with a small manhood would not be 'affected.' Even the *frenulum* of a boy cannot be torn. Many times, parents get to know that their son was having sex when he tells them or when they discover that he has a sexually transmitted infection.

So, if Parliament amends section 138 so that a boy can be defiled, corroboration evidence may not be there to prove the occurrence of the offence. And, if a mistake of doing away with corroboration evidence is made, a lot of innocent women would get jailed. This would be the case especially if the age of defilement is pushed to 18 years and boys become eligible to be defiled too. Since there will be no need for corroboration evidence, a boy ov 17 and half years would tell his story on how he was defiled by a woman or young lady older than him. Because parliament will have graded him as a child, the court will listen to his verbal evidence and convict the woman defiler probably to 15 years imprisonment.

A girl under 16 years is considered incapable of m a k i n g s o u n d d e c i s i o n s t o wa r d s s e x u a l intercourse. This law is there to protect girls because they are a 'weaker' sex and can easily be pressurized or intimidated into sex. Even after intercourse, they may not tell their parents or guardians. The moment defilement is extended to boys, the boy will enjoy the same privileges as a girl. He will cease to give consent to sexual intercourse and any woman or young lady who has intercourse with him does so at her own peril. But is it true that a boy under 18 years, especially one above 16 years, cannot think and protect himself from a woman because he is a weaker sex? In Zambia today, who are busy having intercourse with young girls of 12 and 16 years? Are not boys aged 17, 18 and over? Furthermore, it is a known fact that boys aged between 14 and 18 years have impregnated girls in Zambia. So, when a boy under 18 has intercourse with a girl under 18, what will determine whether one is guilty or not is his or her age. If a boy is older than a girl he has defiled her and if he is younger than her, then she has defiled him. If a boy aged 18 is arrested for defiling a girl under 18, say one who is 14 years, he will have several privileges. He can simply say "Your honour, I am sorry that I failed to control myself, but I am simply a child who knows nothing or very little about sexual intercourse. Everything happened by mistake. Now that I know that what I did was wrong I beg the court to forgive me for my misdeed. The magistrate or the judge, cannot go beyond the boundaries of the law, hence since a boy below 18 will be graded as a child, the judge will order that he be counseled instead of sending him to prison. Meanwhile, the girl he had intercourse with is pregnant and her parents are considering abortion since her sexual organ is not fully developed for her to keep a baby for nine months and deliver successfully.

Before approving that a boy can be defiled, Parliament should consider whether a boy, especially one aged between 16 and 18, is a weaker sex. Failure to do so may render the law on defilement meaningless. For example, a group of boys aged between 16 and 18 years, probably street kids, may simply hold the hands and legs of a young lady then cover her mouth and allow one of their friends to have intercourse with her in such a way that she does not even sustain bruises or have her pants torn. In order to defend themselves, the one who had intercourse with the lady would rush to the nearest police station and report that a woman made him have intercourse with her. He would lie that she gave him sweets that made him have an erection and later invited him to have sex with her. That is a report of defilement and by law that shall be established; the police are supposed to look for the woman and arrest her for defiling a boy under 18 years. Alternatively, he would simply keep quiet; after all it is not an offence in Zambia to fail to report a crime when you are the victim.

The law on defilement is meant to protect girls because they are a weaker sex, and should not be applicable to young and strong boys aged between 16 and 18. These boys are capable of overpowering and raping a woman and they are able to defend themselves if attacked by a woman. Additionally, if the law on defilement is to work well, there must be somebody to blame and this someone cannot be any person other than a male person, boys above 16 years inclusive.

If parliament wishes to protect boys under 18, they must amend the law on indecent assault so that all men, regardless of age, are protected. Also, the same punishment applicable to defilers should be made available for those persons who will commit indecent assault. If it is agreed that a boy under

18 is internationally recognized as a child because Zambia is a signatory to the Convention of the Rights of the Child, then he should enjoy certain privileges like:

a. Not to be detained in custody with men older than him.

b. He should be subjected to a lenient sentence when he commits a sexual offence but definitely not counseling.

c. Upon conviction, he must be sent to a reformatory school or given a community sentence, e.g. cleaning toilets at a hospital.

Removal of the requirement for corroboration evidence

Corroboration evidence is always necessary in order to prove that not only has the crime been committed, but it was also committed by the accused. Corroboration evidence is any evidence that supports the statement of the victim or complainant. Hence, Corroboration evidence needs not be conclusive in itself, but it should be independent evidence that confirms that it is safe to rely on the evidence of the victim.

In as much as Corroboration evidence is needed, it must be appreciated that the Penal Code in section 14(1) indicates that a person under 8 years cannot commit a criminal offence. This is the person who does not require his/her evidence to be strictly corroborated. For how does one expect a one-year old baby to identify the accused? In such instances, all that is needed is Corroboration evidence to indicate the occurrence of the defilement.

Absence of Corroborative evidence may give an accused person a chance to call false witnesses, especially where an alibi is concerned. "Your honour, at that time she is claiming I had intercourse with her, I was at my friend's place and my friend is here to testify on my behalf." In other words, the purpose of corroboration is to strengthen the prosecution's evidence and destroy the possible defences for the accused. If there is no Corroboration evidence, the accused is likely to raise the following defences:

(a) Offence did not occur

If there is no medical Corroboration evidence or any other evidence to indicate that the girl was defiled, the accused can as well allege that the complainant hates him, that was why she organized her daughter to lie that he defiled her. It should be realized that in cases where the hospital is far, traditional mid-wives or elderly women can be asked to check if there was any penetration. At least three independent women who are not related to the girl's family can testify in court on what happened to the girl.

(b) False implication

Mostly, in defilement cases, having said "mostly" this is no longer necessary, the victim will be familiar with the accused. So, the question of identity of the accused may not arise. However, the accused may claim that the girl falsely implicated him, he did not defile her.

Corroboration evidence in regard to false implication will be evidence of opportunity. Did the accused person have an opportunity to commit the offence? When the victim says she was with him at that particular time, what is the accused saying? If he says he was not with her, then where was he? If he admits he was with her, what other clues are there to indicate that he had intercourse with her? That's why medical evidence is important because many times it approximates the time of intercourse. If the time of intercourse coincides with the time when the accused was with the girl, then the court would assume that since the accused was the only person who was with the victim, he utilized that opportunity and had intercourse with the girl.

False implication in defilement has to do with a person who had an opportunity to commit a crime. Therefore, it is a necessary that girls below eight years should always be left in the custody of someone, especially a young lady. Equally, boys below eight years should be left in custody of men and boys. This minimizes the chances of these girls or boys being defiled or indecently assaulted. And if defiled or indecently assaulted, the person who was the custodian of the girl or boy is the first suspect, for he or she had an opportunity to commit defilement or indecent assault.

The movement of girls above eight years but below 12 years should always be monitored. These girls should never be given a chance to mix with old men or boys older than them.

(c) The girl above 16 years

When there is a medical report indicating that intercourse took place and false implication is completely ruled out, the last defence available to the accused is that he believed the girl was above 16 years because she told him so. This evidence is likely to be rejected if the girl appears too young to be 16 years or over.

Nonetheless, if she appears to be around 16, then the court will require Corroboration evidence in regard to her age, evidence like birth certificate and a confirmation from the parents that the girl is below 16.

If Corroboration evidence is done away with, true justice will not prevail. For young girls below 12 years, the only Corroboration evidence needed is one to indicate occurrence of a crime and that the accused had an opportunity to commit the offence so that false implication is ruled out. If the provision requiring Corroboration of the evidence of a girl in defilement cases is removed, the impact will be that a lot of innocent young men will go to jail. A girl would simply say: "Your honour, this man before this court had intercourse with me, even when I was only a child aged 15 years 11 months."And in defence the man would say: "I did not defile her." The girl would then cry out that he did defile her and that a child like her cannot lie.

The law requires that the prosecution should prove beyond all reasonable doubt that the accused person committed defilement. Now it seems this requirement will be vice versa. The accused person, u p o n r e m o v a l o f t h e r e q u i r e m e n t f o r Corroboration evidence, shall be deemed guilty until he proves himself innocent.

Minimum sentence for sexual offences The purpose of sentencing an offender is not only to punish him but also to rehabilitate him/her so that he/she becomes a good citizen after serving the sentence. The minimum sentence should indeed be minimal. While it is that girls should be protected from defilers, it is however noted that the much talked about minimum sentence of 15 years for any defiler is too much. The necessity of the judiciary in sentencing an offender cannot be overemphasized.

It should however be admitted that the girls who are prone to defilement are mostly Zambians and the men who defile them are also mostly Zambians.

Hence, Parliament when enacting the law should protect both. Therefore when setting a minimum sentence, various questions need to be answered.

Questions like: How widespread is the crime in the nation? How many people are likely to be offenders? What are their geographical areas? What is the background of the offence? What is the response of the victims? These questions, if answered correctly, would assist parliament in setting a minimum sentence. A minimum sentence would act as a control measure among judges and magistrate but at the same time, it will make them develop minds. If these educated and dependable people are not flexible in the decisions, then where the 15 years minimum sentence outweighs the evidence given and they are likely to acquit the offender.

This is because they are human beings and have conscience. If they convict where evidence does not allow them to do so, this sense of right and wrong will make them feel guilty for the rest of their lives.

It is believed that a minimum sentence of 15 years will deter others from committing similar offences. This is not true considering the background of the defilement. Even if ignorance of law is not a defence, many Zambians don't understand defilement because government has not explained to them what it is. If a person who stays in Lusaka's

Chaisa compound strongly believes that consensual sexual intercourse with a girl who has reached puberty, even at 13 years, is alright, what about a man in Nabwalya Chiombo's Chiefdom in Mpika District? Nabwalya is a place where it is a miracle for a person to see a motorcar. The only vehicles they know about are land-cruisers driven by game scouts. The girls have the same perception about consensual intercourse just like the young men. They say: "As long as I have reached puberty, I can have sex with my boyfriend."

If it is agreed that the minimum sentence of 15 years imprisonment for defilement is alright, is Parliament saying it is equitable to punish a man who commits defilement in a rural area when he does not even know what the word defilement means? There are people in Zambia who, when you mention defilement, they think it is another drink like Mazoe. Also, is Parliament saying a man who defiles a 15—1/2 year old girl should be given the same sentence like a man who defiles a one-year old baby?

It can be seen that the offence of defilement is wide spread in the nation. A lot of people are offenders and will continue to be so especially in rural areas and compounds. The offence of defilement is not like aggravated robbery which is mostly committed in cities. Defilement is committed in every geographical area of Zambia. Hence a minimum sentence of 15 years for aggravated robbery is justifiable because you can rarely hear of such robbery in rural areas. The background of defilement is hard to break. The response of girls to the crime is very poor. If government has not convinced girls below 16 years, especially those aged 14 to 16, to be reporting any sexual intercourse they may involve themselves in, when Parliament adds a harsh minimum sentence to Section 138, is that when girls will start reporting defilement to their parents or guardians?

If the answer is no, then there must be a formula for determining the sentence for the offender. If defilement consent of a girl is not important, therefore sentencing should be based on age of the victim. The principle should be: the younger the girl, the higher the sentence. This will ensure that each man gets a sentence he asked for or deserves.

The minimum sentences for defilement and indecent assault should be the same so that boys under 16 are also protected just like a girl of the same age is protected.

The proposed legal definitions for the two offences may be as follows:

Legal definition of indecent assault i. Any person who unlawfully and indecently assaults any boy or girl under 16 years or any other person commits a felony and is liable, upon conviction, to imprisonment for life. In case of boys or girls under 16 years, the minimum sentence shall be 1 year. But if the boy or girl is below 14 years, the minimum sentence shall be 5 years.

ii. It shall not be a defence to a charge of indecent assault to prove that a girl or boy under 16 years consented to the act of indecency.

iii. Any person convicted under subsection (i) where the court deems it fit, shall be required to undergo Human Immunodeficiency Virus (HIV) test before he or she is sentenced.

Legal definition of defilement or statutory rape i. Any person who unlawfully has sexual intercourse with any girl under the age of 16 years commits a felony and is liable, upon conviction, to minimum sentence of 1 year or a maximum of life imprisonment. But if the boy or girl is below 14 years, the minimum sentence shall be 5 years.

ii. Any person who attempts to commit the offence in section 138 (i) commits a felony and is liable, upon conviction, to imprisonment for a termnot exceeding 15 years.

iii. Provided that it shall be sufficient defence to any charge under this section if it shall be made to appear to the court before whom the charge shall be brought that the person so charged had reasonable cause to believe, and did in fact believe, that the girl was of or above the age of sixteen.

iv. Any person convicted under subsection (i) shall b e r e q u i r e d t o u n d e r g o H u m a n Immunodeficiency Virus (HIV) test before he is sentenced.

The proposed formula for calculating sentences

The proposed formula for calculating sentences fordefilers and those who have indecently assaulted girls or boys will give a judge or magistrate a flexible mind and an offender will be rewarded for his acts. The formula proposed is:

Sentence: P+ (16—N) + X Where:

Pis the minimum sentence 16 is the statutory age limit for defilement or indecent assault N is the age of the victim
X is any additional period which must be greater than or equal to zero

Examples:
1. If a girl aged 8 is defiled by her father aged 40 years who is HIV positive and the judge wishes to add 100 years, the sentence would be:

Sentence: P+ (16—N) + X
5 + (16 – 8) + 100 (life imprisonment)
Life imprisonment*

*Your mitigation that you are a family man is of no use to this Court because if the courts lets you free, you shall defile other remaining children. Older persons like you must protect all girls below 12 years, and if defiled as long as I am the judge of this court, defilers will be sentenced to life imprisonment. I therefore sentence you to life imprisonment and the sentence begins from the date when you were arrested.

2. If a girl aged 15 ½ years is defiled by a 17 year old young man and the magistrate wishes to add nil years, the sentence would be:

Sentence: P+ (16—N) + X
1 + (16 − 15) + 0
2 years*

*"After hearing your mitigation, I have reminded myself that you are a young person, as such I will give you a lenient community sentence of 2 years. Since you stay in George Compound, you shall be the sanitary orderly at George Clinic."

3. If a lady aged 19 has intercourse with a 13 year old boy and, when sentencing her for indecent assault, the magistrate adds 2 years, the sentence would be:

Sentence: P+ (16—N) + X
5 + (16 − 13) + 2

10 years imprisonment

*"You ladies must learn to protect these boys and not to use them as sexual objects. Did you believe after intercourse he would suddenly become a man and marry you? I therefore sentence you to 10 years imprisonment."

4. If a 20 year old young man has intercourse with a girl aged 12 years and the magistrate wishes to add 11 years, the sentence would be:

Sentence: P+ (16—N) + X
5 + (16 − 12) + 11
20 years imprisonment with hard labour*

*"You can't say you believed the girl was 16 years or over for even when any reasonable person looks at her, he can only conclude that she is below 16 years, this court therefore sentences you to 20 years imprisonment."

Defilement of girls below 12 years should carry stiffer punishment regardless of the defence given by the defiler. The 'animal in man' of older men having intercourse with girls as young as 3 months, should come to an end.

Mostly, these men have sex with teenagers because traditional doctors have told them to do so, so that they can become rich, famous, be able to have children, cast demons or ghosts away, or even get healed of diseases like HIV/AIDS, etc. If it is for sexual gratification, older men would go for ladies.

Unfortunately, there are women who are having intercourse with young boys. It should be realized that a traditional doctor, according to Section 21, is simply a counselor who should be arrested for defilement. It is not always that a counselor, like a traditional doctor, can be given a lesser sentence; he may as well be given a higher sentence than a person he counseled to commit a crime. An intercourse with a girl aged 151/2 years only when you explain to them what defilement is, that is when they would say "then any older man who has sex with a girl below 13 must be sentenced to more than 10 years imprisonment. It is a fact that people have complained against the judiciary over some sentences given to offenders in regard to defilement. And, if any woman is asked: "Do you think it is right for defilers to be sentenced to minimum of 15 years? The answer would be: "In fact, the minimum sentence should be life imprisonment because the courts have been giving very small sentences." If asked "why", the answer would be: "Because the children they defile know nothing about life." If asked further, "Do you understand defilement, madam? Do you know what it is?" The answer will be: "It is a sexual intercourse with a girl who has not reached marriageable age. I mean one who has not reached puberty." Many women who are wishing that defilers should be given a statutory minimum harsh sentence don't even understand what defilement is. What they don't know very well is that their 19 year old son or brother (probably staying in the village) is on his way to prison for 15 years for having intercourse with a girl aged 15 1/2years. Only when you explain to them what defilement means, that is when they would say: "Then any older man who has sex with a girl below 13 must be sentenced to more than 10 years imprisonment". The complaints of these people are respected but let Zambians try the judiciary once more and see if they will not give desirable sentences.

Otherwise regulating them over the way they give sentences by adding a minimum sentence of 15 years will simply provoke them to give offenders harsh sentences which they don't deserve. For example: "At 19, you are a grown-up young man. Therefore, for defiling a girl aged 15 years 11 months and 29 days, I sentence you to 55 years imprisonment with hard labour. If Parliament is not careful but makes emotional amendments to the Penal Code, simply because people have cried out to government, a lot of people are likely to suffer, including relatives and sons and daughters of Parliamentarians.

Rape

It should be admitted that a woman can rape a man.

The only hindrance to her being prosecuted is the necessary corroborative evidence. As a result, it may not be prudent to depart from the traditional English law definition, which Britain distributed to its colonies. If a woman sedates a man and then pushes his organ into hers, she has raped him for she has had sex without his consent.

But where is the evidence to prove that she has raped him? The most convincing evidence is the sperm, which apparently is in her person. If she baths, she is likely to get rid of that evidence. If the doctor examines a man, is he likely to get any evidence? No! The vaginal fluids will have dried up by the time he reaches the hospital. And, without a proper DNAtest, it is most likely that the doctor's opinion will be negative. The medical evidence is even if when the woman rapist used a condom. In rape cases, it is mandatory that penetration, no matter how slight, has to be proved. Consequently, a police officer will fail to prove penetration in the court.

Suppose a man penetrates a woman with an object, which could be a test tube, a bottle, banana, etc., the medical evidence may be readily available to prove penetration. In addition, the object used has to be presented as an evidence in court. This evidence should be applicable to a woman who penetrates a girl's or woman's organ, or a man's anus, without such person's consent. If a woman engages in fellatio activities without the consent of a man, she can be said to have forced the man's organ into her mouth. If such an act is equated to rape, it would be difficult to get medical evidence.

Equally, if a man engages in cunnilingus acts, how will such acts be proved in court? If a woman sucks a man's organ, is the doctor likely to prove that truly the man's penis was sucked? How long will it take for a woman's saliva to dry on the man's organ before he is examined? In short, parliament should enact laws which are capable of being proved, otherwise it is humiliating to the police if efforts to enforce a particular law yield any positive results.

As such, instead of defining rape widely, it is better to enact another offence which does not require medical evidence. In this regard, fellatio and cunnilingus acts, a woman having intercourse with a man without his consent and inserting objects into a woman's or girl's organ or man's anus, should be given another offence. However, the punishment should be similar to rape.

Such an offence could be termed; "Gross indecent assault" and it can be defined as follows:

1. Any person, who without the consent of that person,

a. Causes the penetration of his/her genitalia or anus using a male organ, or

b. With an object penetrates the genitalia or anus of another person, or c. Engages in fellatio and cunnilingus acts with the other person, shall be guilty of an offence termed gross indecent assault and shall be liable to imprisonment for life.

1. In the case of boys or girls under 16 years, it shall not be a defense that the boy or girl consented to indecent assault.

2. The requirement of medical evidence to prove the occurrences mentioned in Subsection (1), shall not be mandatory.

3. Any person convicted under Subsection (1), where the court deems it fit, shall be required to undergo Human Immunodeficiency Virus (HIV) test before he or she is sentenced.

Incest

When amending the law on incest, the biggest word to preserve is consanguinity (blood relationship). Internationally, especially in commonwealth countries, incest is an offence related to blood relationships.

Therefore, if sexual intercourse with an adoptive son or daughter becomes incest, then the universal meaning of incest will be distorted. However, should parliament wish to protect adoptive children from their non— biological parents, it should enact a law to protect them so that the universal image of incest among commonwealth countries is maintained. In fact, it is not only adoptive children or step-children who are bound to be sexually abused.

It is morally wrong for a grown –up stepson to have intercourse with his stepmother. Neither is it right for a man to have intercourse with a niece to his wife who is above 16 years. It should also be known that if these people are below 16 years, then defilement or indecent assault will be applicable. If they are above 16 and unwillingly consent to sex because they are intimidated, Section 132(b) will apply. If however, they are above 16 years and they consent to sex, as at now, there is no offence that such people can be charged with. You cannot arrest a woman for having intercourse with her 21-year old stepson. So parliament should move forward and enact a law that shall see to it that those having i n t e r c o u r s e w i t h a d o p t i v e c h i l d r e n a n d stepchildren are punished for it is morally wrong to do so. If it is in the interest of Parliament to protect these people, a new law may read as follows:

Any person above the age of 16 years who unlawfully and carnally knows any person who to his or her knowledge is not a blood relationship but they stay together or are regarded as a family and that person is a stepfather, stepmother, adopted son, adopted daughter, stepson, stepdaughter, adopted sister, adopted brother, niece or nephew to uncle's wife or aunt's husband, commits a felony termed gross indecent acts among family members and liable upon conviction to life imprisonment.

Consent of either party shall not be a defence to the charge of gross indecent acts among family members.

Provocation

A few men accused of rape have used provocation as a defence. For example:

Magistrate: Accused, do you plead guilty or not guilty to the charge of rape? Accused: I plead guilty your honour.

Magistrate: Why do you plead guilty? Accused: Because it is true I raped her. Magistrate: What made you rape her? Accused: I was provoked.

Magistrate: What do you mean?

Accused: I mean her dressing was provocative such that I lost self-control and ended up forcing her into sex.

Instead of men claiming to have been provoked, parliament should go a step further and include "indecent exposure" in the Penal Code. Thus, persons who expose their nakedness will be charged with such an offence. Indecent exposure is crime of showing one's private or sexually alluring sensitive parts to other people in the public place. Indecent exposure does not only mean being naked in a public place, it also means being indecently dressed. Generally, for the sake of morality, the following parts of woman's body need not to be exposed in the public:

i. The navel and the stomach ii. The breast iii. The thigh: this is the area between the top part of the knee and the hip.

iv. The buttocks: these are the two round soft parts at the top of a person's legs, if the people are able to see the pants or G-strings, then buttocks are exposed.

How can indecent exposure be if included in the penal code?

Maybe, it would be:

Any person who unlawfully or indecently exposes himself or herself in a public place, is guilty of a misdemeanour (termed indecent exposure) and shall be liable to one-year imprisonment or a fine, or to both: In the above definition, unlawfully means not allowed by law. Therefore activities that may be deemed to be acts of indecency may not actually constitute an offence. A public place is one where people go to or are likely to go to. Right of admission to such a place is not necessary. A person is a reasonable human being able to see, hence insane and totally blind people cannot be witnesses to acts of indecency.

Therefore, indecent exposure is committed mostly by exposing one's body indecently. For the offence to be committed: i The accused has to be in a public place, and ii. His or her, indecency should be seen by a person or two.

Many times, indecent exposure is thought to be an offence committed against a member of the opposite sex. This is not true as men can also report their fellow man if he undresses in their presence. Also, a private or restricted place may turn out to be a public place, as long as people are able to go there. For example, if A, masturbates in a garage that is marked 'restricted place' he commits an offence if his work mates find him indecently exposed.

The general understanding is that, for any person to be accused of indecent exposure, his or her act or acts should extremely go beyond the limit of what is morally or legally accepted decency in a community, and such act or acts should offend an ordinary person.

To accuse any person of indecent exposure, reasonable judgement is required, as to the acceptable norms of a particular situation. For example, people who may appear indecently dressed at a swimming pool have not indecently exposed themselves to the public. Even if, it is only one person swimming and that person is only in pants, he/she has not indecently exposed the body. However, the same person if he/she walks into a shop and removes the clothes such would have committed the offence.

Dramatists on stage are not liable for prosecution for indecent exposure if in an attempt to dramatize a situation, for example, how prostitutes dress and parade the streets at night, they indecently exposes their bodies. Equally, participants at games or sports like bodybuilding, beauty pageant, etc, are not liable for indecent dressing. However, a golfer who goes to play golf whilst indecently dressed would have indecently exposed himself.

Hence, the time at which the offence is deemed to have been committed, the place where a person indecently exposed the body and the situation in which the offence was committed, are very important things to consider before a person is accused of indecent exposure.

Indecent exposure in Zambia, though not an offence, is common among women. Women can be deemed to have committed the offence through dressing, provided a good number of people condemn such dressing and term it as indecent exposure, or, make comments like, 'Dressing like that is as good as walking naked.' 'It is difficult to tell whether one is fit to be called a human being or not. Look at how indecently dressed she is!' If the Zambian culture demands that people must be decently dressed, any person who dresses indecently would have indecently exposed the body.

Side effects of indecent exposure are extremely worrisome and have made many men to commit sexual offences.

Here are examples:

(1) A, a married man and a father of two children, parked his BMW car at the post office in order to check for letters. As he walked into the

building, he saw a very beautiful lady. She had almost exposed her body; her miniskirt, that was half way her knee and her see—through blouse, exposed her fat and nice legs and teacup shaped breasts. On approximating, she looked 19 years old. This created a lot of imagination and a desire for sexual intercourse. Soon, he developed an erection. Knowing that he was married to a housewife, he quickly drove home. To his disappointment, his wife was not at home, but C, a 15-year-old niece to his wife, was around. When he asked where his wife was, she emerged from her bedroom with only a towel wrapped around her waist. This exposed her niece's body. This did not only increase his desire, but also made him to force the girl into sex, after which the helpless girl remained lying in bed.

When her aunt came back, she did not tell her what has transpired. Unfortunately, she became pregnant. This embarrassed the family. The man was later arrested for defilement. However, like in many such cases, C withdrew the case because A was a breadwinner and if sent to jail, the family would starve to death. Regardless of the girl's mercy, her aunt failed to understand that her husband forced C into sex. She thought C always had sex with A, so she was sent to her grandparents since she had no parent to go to as she was an orphan.

It is evident that A could not have defiled C, if an indecently dressed woman did not catalyze his decision. Some men, after seeing an indecently dressed woman, have rushed home hoping to have sex with their wives but only to end up committing incest.

Also, because of the indecent exposure of ladies, men have ended up contracting HIV/AIDS.

(2) X was a manager in a well-paying company.

After the transfer of his secretary Q, Z a very beautiful lady with a nice figure, was employed. She was straight from college.

Unlike his former secretary who was always dressed decently, Z always dressed in 20—centimetres above-the-knee miniskirt. X felt the urge to warn Z about her dressing but felt no need to do so. A few weeks later, he started imagining how he could feel if he had sex with her. He then proposed to Z and assured her promotion immediately after probation. Knowing that X was the only way to her job success, she faithfully accepted the proposal despite the fact that she knew X was married. They started having sex and soon abandoned the use of condoms. A year after, X learnt that Z's ex-boyfriend died of tuberculosis and diarrhea. He did an HIV test, and he tested positive. X regretted that he accepted Z as his secretary and later proposed to her.

It seems X had no intention to propose to Z, but her indecent exposure made him see what he was not supposed to see. This made his heart thump each day that he saw her. If Z was decently dressed, the sexual relationship could not have happened, and X could not have contracted the deadly disease.

Furthermore, indecent exposure has landed many ladies and girls in problems of sexual abuse and illegitimate children.

(3) X, a very beautiful 20-year-old lady, always used to dress indecently. Her mother, Y, warned her several times that her dressing was not promoting morality in the neighbourhood, but X said: 'Mother how will men admire me if I don't expose my nice body to them? Maybe you don't want me married.'

One day, she dressed in a hipster that made her buttocks dance as she walked. She also put on a see—through crop top that exposed her navel and stomach and made her pinpointed breasts to be visible and went to Arcades Shopping Complex.

Whilst there, Z, a handsome man aged 24 years admired and proposed to her. When she agreed, he said to himself, 'She is proper T-bone, I will feast on her.'

When Y told X that she did not like Z, X said, 'Mum, you don't know what you are talking about. Z has a car, a nice job, cash and clothes. He bought me an expensive cell phone and gives me a lot of money.' However, when X told Z that she was pregnant he told her to mind her own business. That was how X was abandoned. She gave birth to a baby girl and Z never bought even a napkin. Her mother reminded her that if she was not dressing indecently, she would not have lost her purity to Z and, worse still, ending up with an illegitimate child. 'Men who go for indecently dressed women, only follow sex and not marriage,' Y informed her daughter.

It is the duty of the government to protect citizens from unlawful activities and they can only do so by enacting laws. <u>When an immoral conduct is</u> <u>as prevalent as indecent exposure, it is better to</u> <u>protect the people.</u> <u>Again</u> <u>its consequences maybe</u> <u>the mode of punishment, that is, if Parliament</u> <u>considers indecent exposure as an offence, is to</u> <u>charge the offender</u> <u>admission of guilty fee of</u> K 5 0 0, 0 0 0 o r o n i n d i c t m e n t, t o o n e—y e a r <u>imprisonment. Then, people can see how many</u> <u>women can</u> <u>dress indecently, get arrested and pay</u> <u>the said fine, after which they go</u> <u>and dress</u> <u>indecently again.</u>

Finally, it should be remembered that police would not enforce a law that does not exist. Unless, Parliament enacts the law, indecent exposure will never be an offence. After enactment of indecent exposure law, the police will arrest: any woman who unlawfully exposes either the navel or her breasts or both, in public; any woman or girl wearing hipsters in public that do not cover her buttocks in full, that is, a hipster not reaching the waist; any woman wearing a miniskirt in public. A miniskirt is a skirt that does not cover the thighs completely; it leaves a large proportion of the thigh exposed. It should be known that wearing tight cloths like, leggings and tight blouses, which do not expose the mentioned parts, does not amount to indecent exposure. Also, exposing shoulders or the back or both is not indecent exposure. Back means the part of a woman's body that is on the opposite side to the chest and it extends from the lower neck to the waist. But certainly, wearing of a crop top in public is indecent exposure for it will expose the woman's navel and stomach. Men should also be arrested if they unlawfully expose their buttocks to the public.

Synopsis

Though a man can be raped, it is not necessary that a law on rape of men be enacted. Men and boys can be protected by the law on indecent assault.

Indecent exposure is an offence that has more to do with showing one's private parts. Generally, it is a crime of showing parts of the body that are supposed to be properly covered. Indecent exposure is not an offence in Zambia.

CHAPTER 8

Vsu, Police Statistics on Sexual Offences and Sentencing of Offenders

VSU, POLICE STATISTICS ON SEXUAL OFFENCES AND SENTENCING OF OFFENDERS

The Birth Of Victim Support Unit (VSU)

The VSU was formed in 1994. However, its operation actively started in 1997. By mid- 1998, most police stations had established offices for VSU. The following scenario was partly why the VSU was formed.

A victim of rape arrived at the Inquires office and she found six police officers and eight people who had different complaints. She approached an officer who had no client.

The birth of VSU was, partly, ignited by such conduct of police officers. It was purely a problem of specialization. Police officers had various complaints of offences to deal with, hence, they lacked specialization. The changing of the name from Zambia Police Force to Zambia Police Service, though the change is not legally recognized by Parliament, brought various changes including the formation of VSU. However, the minds of police officers were not immediately changed; it was a gradual process.

Police officers now understand that they have to properly offer their services to the people and not to deal with them with force.

The Zambia Police Service came with its own programmes to promote efficiency and effectiveness in the service. One of these programmes was to stop recruiting grade nines as police officers and start recruiting grade twelve with division one or two certificates only. Also, Zambia Police Service recognized the intellectual demand behind service work, hence some officers were sent to various colleges and universities. As though that was not enough, university graduates were also being recruited.

Specialization is now found in all provincial headquarters of Zambia. For example, in each provincial divisional headquarters, the Criminal Investigations Department (CID), is divided into sections, namely: frauds, homicide, housebreaking/ burglary and theft, 'anti-robbery' squad, etc.

This means, complaints need not pass through the inquiries office, instead, they should go straight to the section related to the complaint. If it is a forged cheque, it is handled by the anti-frauds sections mentioned above which are found only at provincial level, VSU offices are found at each police station in Zambia, no matter how remote a station may be. And, brilliant officers have been chosen to work in the VSU. Hence, because of its importance, VSU is not a section but a minor department, just like prosecution and traffic, under the Community Service Department (CSD). As the name implies, the common goal of the department is to support victims of sexual crimes and those of property grabbing, spouse battering and victimization of elders.

All victims of sexual offences are supposed to enjoy the right to confidentiality and privacy. This is well known to police officers working in the VSU. Even if there is not enough manpower at a station in the VSU office, the client has the right to privacy. "Officer, may I talk to you privately. You see my niece has been defiled by my husband." Police officers in the VSU are friendly and are ready to welcome complaints.

Despite a good department in place, officers face one major drawback: transport. Lack of transport has made people to complain against the VSU offices' performance. At times, police officers use their money to take victim to the hospital. This is not uncommon, especially in Lusaka where University Teaching Hospital is relied upon as the major health centre to handle rape and defilement cases. Maybe the solution is for donors to assist the VSU offices with transport, especially in Lusaka and the Copperbelt provinces where there are more than one police station in a town.

Transport has made many victims of sexual offences not to report cases to the VSU as many Zambians are poor and cannot afford transport to and from the hospital. "When my niece was raped, the police told us that there was no transport. They were relying on a Central Police Station vehicle, which apparently had broken-down. So I ended up booking a car and it was very expensive. So Mrs. Tembo, if you have no money don't even bother going to the police. If your daughter can't get examined within 24 hours she will be assumed not to have been raped. I tell you, you will see time passing without the police taking her to the hospital. "The other problem is office accommodation. This is vital as confidentiality and privacy depend on it. Many VSU offices are very small, whilst others are shared with other departments.

Law enforcement statistics on sexual offences

Law enforcement statistics are based on reported cases. It is from reported cases that investigations commence and, if possible, arrests made. The procedure is that when a complaint is made, such a case is included among reported cases. When the suspect is arrested for the offence he has committed, he becomes an accused person, and is supposed to be taken to court together with his case record. When the accused pleads guilty to a charge or he is found guilty of the offence and sentenced, he becomes a convict or a prisoner. The disposed case is then recorded among convictions. If the accused is acquitted, the case is recorded among acquittals. The complainant can withdraw a case. Withdrawal of cases can be done at the police station or at the court. Also, it should be realized that some cases are closed at the police station or at the court. Also, it should be realized that some cases can be dropped at the police station due to insufficient evidence or upon the death of witnesses (especially the complainant) or the accused. Some cases may be pending because the police have not finished gathering evidence or can be carried forward to the next year.

Reported cases indicate the occurrence of a particular sexual offence in Zambia. A big figure means that there is a high prevalence of such an offence in the country. This could be due to ignorance of the law by people who may be perpetrators of sexual offences who are not educated on what constitutes the crime or the victims are not fully aware of the crime, hence, they do not rush to the police to report. It is also possible that due to the social stigma of sexual offences, especially rape, defilement, incest, bestiality and sodomy, a victim may fail to report despite being aware that what has been done to her or him is a criminal offence.

BAR CHART FOR DEFILEMENT CASES

REPORTED TO THE POLICE BETWEEN 2009 AND 2012

The bar chart of defilement cases reported between 2009 and 2012 may mean an increase in defilement cases. This may simply mean that parents and guardians were but now are reporting defilement cases. It may also mean that parents have stopped applying the traditional rule of considering a girl aged between 13 and 16, if she willingly has sex with a man, as a 'stupid' girl, hence admonishing her without reporting the defiler to the police.

Additionally, it may mean that previously, girls were not telling their guardians and parents that they consented to sex; defilement has a long history and many times people used to avoid reporting cases to the police. It is a hidden truth that most women surviving today, willingly had sex before they attained the age of 16.

More campaigns should be done to sensitize not only the would-be victims but also the would-be perpetrators on the dangers of defilement to society and the punishment thereafter.

Synopsis

The VSU brought specialization in the Zambia Police Service and improved efficiency in the way police officers dealt with sexual offences. The principle of sentencing of a sexual offender is: In defilement, the lower the age of the girl, the higher the sentence.

In rape, it all depends upon the quality of evidence available and the circumstances in which the rape was committed.

Sexual offences, especially rape and defilement, are contributing to high levels of HIV/AIDS in the country.

Chiefs and subjects, village headmen and pupils should be educated on sexual offences.

CHAPTER 9

Sexual Offences in other Commonwealth Countries

Funso

Sexual Offence In Botswana

Sexual offences in Botswana are stated in Chapter 08:01of the Laws of Botswana. Chapter 08:01 is the Penal Code of Botswana.

Rape

Section 141: Definition of rape (5 of 1998, s 2.)

Any person who has unlawful carnal knowledge of another person, or who causes the penetration of a sexual organ or instrument, of whatever nature, into the person of another for the purposes of sexual gratification, or who cause the penetration of another persons' sexual organ into his or her person, without the consent of such other person, or with such persons' consent, if the consent is obtained by

a. force, or

b. means of threats or intimidation of any kind, or

c. by fear of bodily harm, or

d. by means of false representation as to the nature of the act, or SEXUAL OFFENCE IN BOTSWANA

Sexual offences in Botswana are stated in Chapter 08:01of the Laws of Botswana. Chapter 08:01 is the Penal Code of Botswana.

Rape

Section 141: Definition of rape (5 of 1998, s 2.)

Any person who has unlawful carnal knowledge of another person, or who causes the penetration of a sexual organ or instrument, of whatever nature, into the person of another for the purposes of sexual gratification, or who cause the penetration of another persons' sexual organ into his or her person, without the consent of such other person, or with such persons' consent, if the consent is obtained by

a. force, or

b. means of threats or intimidation of any kind, or

c. by fear of bodily harm, or

d. by means of false representation as to the nature of the act, or capacity to make that choice.

Section 142: Punishment for rape (5 of 1998, s 3.)

1. Any person who is charged with the offence of rape shall-

i. not be entitled to be granted bail; and

ii. Subject to subsections (2) and (4), upon conviction be sentenced to a minimum term of 10 years' imprisonment or to a maximum of life imprisonment.

1. Where an act of rape is attended by violence resulting in injury to the victim, the person convicted of the act of rape shall be sentenced to a minimum term of 15 years' imprisonment or to a maximum term of life imprisonment with or without corporal punishment.

2. Any person convicted of rape shall be required to undergo a Human Immune-system Virus test before he or she sentenced by the court.

3. Any person who is convicted under subsection

(1) or subsection (2) and whose test for the Human Immune—system Virus under subsection (3) is positive shall be sentenced –

a. to a minimum term of 15 years' imprisonment or to a maximum term of life imprisonment with corporal punishment, where it is proved that such person was unaware of being Human Immune—system Virus positive; or b. to a minimum term of 20 years' imprisonment or to a maximum term of life imprisonment with corporal punishment, where it is a proved that on a balance of probabilities such person was aware of being Human Immune-system Virus positive.

1. Any person convicted and sentenced for the offence of rape shall not have the sentence imposed run con—currently with any other sentence whether the other sentence be for the offence of rape or any other offence.

A person charged with rape cannot be given bail or police bond. Such a person if found guilty, must undergo an HIV test so that if he/she is positive and was not aware of his/her status, the minimum sentence should be 15 years. If he/she is found HIV positive and that he/she was aware of his/her status, the minimum sentence is 20 years. A person convicted of rape, who also had committed other offences or has committed many rapes, he/she shall have his/her sentence run consecutively (one sentence after another) and not concurrently (at the same time). So a woman, sentenced for rape in circumstances where she sedated a man and had intercourse with him and when he woke up he found her having sex with him and as he tried to stop her, she strangled and them beat him up, will have her sentence for rape and assault run consecutively. If, say, she is given 20 years for rape and 5 years for assault, she will first serve the sentence for rape then start the sentence for assault. The total number of years will come to 25 years. If the sentence is 'swallowed' by the bigger sentence, such that she can only serve 20 years, it is serving the sentences concurrently but this is not the law of Botswana.

Defilement

Section 147: Defilement of person under 16 years

(5 of 1998, s, 8.)

1. Any person who unlawfully and carnally knows any girl under the age of 16 years is guilty of an offence and on conviction shall be sentenced to

a minimum term of 10 years' imprisonment or to a maximum term of life imprisonment.

2. Any person convicted under subsection (1) shall be required to undergo a Human Immune-system Virus test before he or she sentenced is by the court.

3. Any person who is convicted under subsection (1) and whose test for the Human Immune-system Virus under subsection (2) is positive shall be sentenced to a—a. minimum term of 15 years' imprisonment or to a maximum term of life imprisonment with or without corporal punishment, where it is proved that such person was unaware of being Human Immune-system Virus positive; or b. minimum term of 20 years' imprisonment or to a maximum term of life imprisonment with or without corporal punishment, where it is proved that on a balance of probabilities such person was aware of being Human Immune-system Virus positive.

1. Any person who attempts to have unlawful carnal knowledge of any person under the age of 16 years is guilty of an offence and is liable to imprisonment for a term not exceeding 14 years, with or without corporal punishment.

2. It shall be a sufficient defense to any charge under this section if it appears to the court before whom the charge is brought that the person so charged had reasonable cause to believe and did in fact believe that the person was of or above the age of 16 years or was such charged person's spouse.

The law on defilement in Botswana is the same as in Zambia, except that in Botswana, if found guilty, the accused has to undergo an HIV test. If the accused is found positive, the minimum sentence is increased. Even in Botswana, for defilement to suffice there must be: i. Sexual intercourse (carnal knowledge) and it includes even a slightest penetration. ii. That sexual act should be with a girl under 16 year's iii. The consent of a girl, whether express (e.g. where a girl under 16 removes all her clothes and invites a man to have sex with her) or implied (e.g. Where a man removes her clothes or makes her remove her clothes by force or any other means), is not important.

iv. The sexual act must be unlawful (not in marriage).

Note that, as discussed in Chapter one, a woman can commit defilement by being an abettor, procurer, counsellor or aider. Chapter four is very relevant. If she uses any instrument to penetrate a girl e.g. a test tube, with or without her consent she can be arrested for rape or indecent assault.

Just like in Zambia, a man having sex with a girl under 16 years to whom he is lawfully married does not commit defilement or statutory rape in Botswana. Section 147 (5) " . . . was such charged person's spouse," refers.

Indecent assault

Section 146: Indecent assault (5 of 1998, s.7 (a))

1. Any person who unlawfully and indecently assaults any person is guilty of an offence and is liable to imprisonment for a term not exceeding seven years, with or without corporal punishment.

The explanation of indecent assault is as contained in Chapter 4 except that under Botswana Penal Code, a male person regardless of age can be indecently assaulted by a woman.

Section 168: Incest (5 of 1998, s.23)

1. Any person who knowingly has carnal knowledge of another person, knowing that person to be his or her grandchild, child, brother, sister or parent, is guilty of an offence and is liable to imprisonment for a term not exceeding five years.

Provided that if it is alleged in the indictment or summons and proved that the person of whom carnal knowledge was had is under the age of 16 years, the offender shall be liable to imprisonment for life.

2. It is Immaterial that the carnal knowledge was had with the consent of the person of whom carnal knowledge was had.

Section 169: Incest by females (5 of 1998, s.23)

Any female person of or above the age of sixteen years who with consent permits her grandfather, father, brother, or son to have carnal knowledge of her (knowing him to be her grandfather, father, brother, or son, as the case may be) is guilty of a felony and is liable to imprisonment for five years.

Section 170: Test of relationship

In Sections 168 and 169 the expressions "brother " and "sister " respectively include half-brother and half-sister, and the provision of the said sections shall apply whether the relationship between the person charged with an offence and the person with whom the offence is alleged to have been committed is or is not traced through lawful wedlock.

Section 164: Unnatural offences (5 of 1998, s.21)

Any person who – a. has carnal knowledge of any person against the order of nature; or a. has carnal knowledge of an animal; or b. permits a male person to have carnal knowledge of him or her against the order of nature is guilty of an offence and is liable to imprisonment for a term not exceeding 7 years.

Sexual Offences In Malawi

Sexual offences in Malawi are defined in Chapter 07:01 of the Laws of Malawi. Chapter 07:01 is the Penal Code of Malawi.

Rape

Section 132: Definition of rape. (Rape is defined in the same way as it is defined in Zambia. Surprisingly it is also Section 132)

Funso

Any person who has unlawful carnal knowledge of a woman or girl without her consent or with her consent, if the consent is obtained by

a. *force, or*

b. *means of threats or intimidation of any kind, or*

c. *by fear of bodily harm, or*

d. *by means of false representation as to the nature or the act, or*

e. *in case of a married woman by personating her husband, is guilty of a felony termed 'rape'.*

Section 133: Punishment for rape

Any person who commits the offence of rape shall be liable to be punished with death or with imprisonment for life, with or without corporal punishment.

Defilement

Section 138: Defilement of girls under 13 years

1. Any person who unlawfully and carnally knows any girl under the age of 13 years shall be guilty of a felony and shall be liable to imprisonment for life, with or without corporal punishment.

2. Provided that it shall be a sufficient defence to any charge under this section if it shall be made to appear to the court before whom the charge shall be brought that the person so charged had reasonable cause to believe, and did in fact believe, that the girl was of or above the age of thirteen.

The definition of defilement in Malawi is similar to the Zambian definition. The only difference is the age of consent to sex which is fixed at 13 years. Hopefully, Malawi will soon increase the age of consent to sexual intercourse by girls and make it an offence for any man to have sex with a girl under 16 years with or without her consent.

With regard to incest and indecent assault on females, the definitions are the same in Malawi and Zambia, as long as the age of 13 years is observed. Unnatural offences are defined in the same way as in Zambia.

Sexual Offences In Kenya

Sexual offences in Kenya are defined in Chapter 63 of the Laws of Kenya. Chapter 63 is the Penal Code of Kenya.

Rape

Section 139: Definition of rape (the definition is the same as in Zambia word by word. As such chapter three is vital to Kenyans)

Any person who has unlawful carnal knowledge of a woman or girl, without her consent, or with her consent if the consent is obtained by force or by means of threats or intimidation of any kind, or by fear of bodily harm. or by means of false representation as to the nature of the act, or, in the case of a married woman, by personating her husband, is guilty of the felony termed rape.

Defilement

Section 145: Defilement of girls under 14 years

1. Any person who unlawful and carnally knows any girl under the age of fourteen (14) years is guilty of a felony and is liable to imprisonment with hard labour for fourteen years together with corporal punishment.

2. Any person who attempts to have unlawful carnal knowledge of a girl under the age of fourteen (14) years is guilty of a felony and is liable to imprisonment with hard labour f o r f i v e years, with or without corporal punishment.

Provided that it shall be a sufficient defence to any charge under this section if it is made to appear to the court before whom the charge is brought that the person so charged had reasonable cause to believe and did in fact believe that the girl was of or above the age of fourteen (14) years or was his wife.

Defilement in Kenya is just like in Zambia, except that the age of consent to sex by a girl is 14 years whilst in Zambia it is 16. The Kenyan Government is in the process of increasing the age of consent to sexual intercourse to age 16 one case is important here, as the provision to Section 145 (2) reads as follows:" . . . did in fact believe that the girl was of or above the age of fourteen (14) years or was his wife."As such, for a Kenyan to claim that he is validly married to a girl under 14 years, he must prove that he married the girl according to customary law as English law does not promote marriage of girls under 16 years.

Other sexual offences like: indecent assault on boys, indecent assault on females, unnatural offences are defined just like in Zambia.

Sexual Offences In Zimbabwe

The law relating to sexual offences is contained in Sexual Offences Act 2001. This Act is Chapter 9:21 of the Laws of Zimbabwe and it clearly defines statutory rape (or defilement), rape and indecent assault. In the Act:

i. "Young person" means a boy or girl under the age of 16 years.

ii. "HIV" means Human Immunodeficiency

Virus

iii. "Extra-marital sexual intercourse" means sexual intercourse otherwise than between husband and wife. It is the same as unlawful carnal knowledge.

Section three of the Sexual Offences Act 2001 looks at extra-marital sexual intercourse or indecent act committed with a young person. According to the Zambian Criminal Law, this is explained in Chapter four of this book as defilement and indecent assault.

Section 3: Extra-marital intercourse or immoral or indecent act committed with young person

1 Subject to subsection (2), any person who—

(a) Has extra-marital sexual intercourse with a young person; or (b) Commits an immoral or indecent act with or upon a young person; or

(c) solicits or entices a young person to have extra—marital sexual intercourse with him or to commit an immoral or indecent act; Shall be guilty of an offence and liable, subject to section sixteen, to a fine not exceeding fifty thousand dollars or to imprisonment for a period not exceeding ten years or to both such fine and such imprisonment.

Defilement in Kenya is just like in Zambia, except that the age of consent to sex by a girl is 14 years whilst in Zambia it is 16. The Kenyan Government is in the process of increasing the age of consent to sexual intercourse to age 16, one case is an important case here as the proviso to Section 145 (2) reads as follows: " . . . did in fact believe that the girl was of or above the age of fourteen (14) years or was his wife."As such for a Kenyan to claim that he is validly married to a girl under 14 years, he must prove that he married the girl according to customary law as English law does not promote marriage of girls under 16 years.

Other sexual offences like: indecent assault on boys, indecent assault on females, unnatural offences are defined just like in Zambia.

Sexual Offences In Zimbabwe

The law relating to sexual offences is contained in Sexual Offences Act 2001. This Act S Chapter 9:21 of the Laws of Zimbabwe and it clearly defines statutory rape (or defilement), rape and indecent assault. In the Act:

i. "Young person" means a boy or girl under the age of 16 years. ii. "HIV" means Human Immunodeficiency

Virus iii. "Extra-marital sexual intercourse" means sexual intercourse otherwise than between husband and wife. It is the same as unlawful carnal knowledge.

Section three of the Sexual Offences Act 2001 looks at extra-marital sexual intercourse or indecent act committed with a young person. According to the Zambian Criminal Law, this is explained in Chapter four of this book as defilement and indecent assault.

Section 3: Extra-marital sexual intercourse or indecent act committed with young person

1. Subject to subsection (2), any person who—

a. Has extra-marital sexual intercourse with a young person; or b. Commits an immoral or indecent act with or upon a young person; or c. Solicits or entices a young person to have extra—marital sexual intercourse with him or to commit an immoral or indecent act;

Shall be guilty of an offence and liable, subject to section sixteen, to a fine not exceeding fifty thousand dollars or to imprisonment for a period not exceeding ten years or to both such fine and such imprisonment.

1. It shall be a defence to a charge under subsection (1) for the accused person to satisfy the court that— a. he was under the age of sixteen years at the time of the alleged offence; or b. he had reasonable cause to believe that the young person concerned was of or over the age of sixteen years at the time of the alleged offence.

In Zimbabwe a boy or girl under 16 years of age can be statutorily raped or defiled. This is because section three of theAct makes it unlawful for any person to have sexual intercourse with a boy or girl less than 16 years with or without his/her consent.

Section 3(2) is the defence available to an accused charged with extra—marital sexual intercourse or indecent act committed with a boy or girl under 16 years. The defence is that:

> Accused is a boy under 16 years then he is not guilty of extra-marital sexual intercourse or indecent act.

> is over 16 years but had reasonable cause to believe that the young person concerned was of or over the age of 16 years then he is not guilty of extra—material sexual intercourse or indecent act, that is, defilement (statutory rape) or indecent assault.

Even if the proviso is there, it is not fair for a young man who has sex with a girl under 16, say who is 15 years, to simply tell the court that he had reasonable cause to believe that the girl was of or over the age 16 years at the time he had intercourse with her. The proviso works well where the accused gives reason why he believed the girl was over 16 years. As such, without doubt, the intention of Parliament was to make any man arrested under Section three to give reasons why he believed the girl was aged 16 or over, at the time of intercourse.

The proviso only refers to 'he'. In this context, Parliament's intention was not to expressly punish females who contravene Section 3(1) without giving them a chance to rely on the statutory defense. According to the Oxford Advanced Learners Dictionary, 'he' has two meaning. (1) 'He' means a male person or animal that has already been mentioned or is early identified. (2) 'He' also means a person, male or female whose sex is not stated or known. The Golden rule of interpreting a statute states that where a word has more than one meaning the court will adopt the one which is not illogical in order to achieve justice. As such, "he" in the Act means both male and female persons; it does not only refer to men. If this is the law, then if a girl aged 15½ years willingly or voluntarily has sex with a 13-year—old boy, then she should rely on Section 3(2)(a).As such, the court will acquit her as she has not committed the offence of extra-marital sexual intercourse with a young person. Equally, if a lady is aged 20 and a boy aged 15½ years consents to sexual intercourse with her when arrested for extra-marital sexual intercourse with a young person, she can rely on the statutory defense under Section 3(2)(b). She could say she had reasonable cause to believe that the boy in question was of or over the age of sixteen years at the time of intercourse because of reasons A, B, C and D.

The fact that the accused person for extra-marital sexual intercourse with a young person (or defilement or statutory rape) is permitted to rely on the proviso under Section 3(2), should not make girls and boys under 16 years to be having indiscriminate sex with just anybody. There is an age limited at which the proviso cannot be relied upon.

Section 23 states that: "Consent by young person is no defense in certain circumstances." Section 23(2) reads:

"A young person under the age of twelve years shall be deemed incapable of consenting to sexual intercourse or a sexual act."

As such a person under the age of 12 years is incapable of consenting to sexual intercourse or any sexual act. In this case, a sexual act means anal intercourse or, engaging in fellatio or cunnilingus. Fellatio means the acts of touching a man's penis with the lips and tongue to give sexual pleasure and cunnilingus means the act of touching a woman's sexual organs with the mouth and tongue to give sexual pleasure. In Zimbabwe, just like in Zambia, according to Section 22 of the Sexual Offences Acts, a boy under 12 years is presumed incapable of committing sexual offence, whether vaginal or anal intercourse .

Marriage with girls under 14 years in Zimbabwe Section 21: Presumption regarding marriage "Whenever in any prosecution under this Act the question is in issue whether any sexual intercourse between two persons was extra-marital, the persons shall be deemed not to have been married at the time of such intercourse, unless the contrary is proved."

". . . The persons shall be deemed not to have been married at the time of such intercourse, unless the contrary is proved."

This means that the person arrested for extra—marital sexual intercourse with a young person, which is unlawful sexual intercourse or defilement or statutory rape, should prove that he/she was legally married to the victim otherwise he/she should be convicted. It should be presumed that marriage where a lady or girl is married to a boy under 16 years is rare or non-existent. However, it is common to see a man married to a girl under 16years. If a man is arrested for extra-marital intercourse with a girl under 16 years when he is married to her, he must prove that he is truly married to the girl otherwise the court will consider him not to be married to the girl. Since English law, which many British colonies like Zimbabwe inherited, does not support marriage of girls under 16 years, such man can only be married according to the customary law of the area or tribe. For example he can claim that he is validly married to such a girl as he married her according to Customary Law of the Shonas, that is, if a girl is Shona by tribe. In short the Rex versus Chinjamba case and its analysis is relevant here. In fact, Chapter four of this book is useful to Zimbabweans.

Section 4: Extra—marital sexual intercourse or immoral or indecent act committed with intellectually handicapped person.

1. in this section-"intellectually handicapped person" means a person who is mentally disordered or intellectually handicapped, as defined in section 2 of the Mental Health Act [Chapter 15:12).

2. Subject to subsection (3), any person who-

a. Has extra-marital sexual intercourse with an intellectually handicapped person: or

b. Commits an immoral or indecent act

c. Solicits or entices an intellectually handicapped person to have extra marital sexual intercourse with him or to commit an immoral or indecent act; shall be guilty of an offence and liable, subject to section sixteen, to a fine not exceeding fifty thousand dollars or to imprisonment for a period not exceeding ten years or to both such fine and such imprisonment.

1. It shall be a defense to a charge under subsection (2) for the accused person to satisfy the court that he did not know that the person to or

with whom he committed the act alleged in the charge was intellectually handicapped.

The law under section 4 is discussed in chapter three under the heading: "Consent of a person of unsound mind."

Rape

Rape is discussed under Section 8 of the Sexual Offences Act 2001 of the laws of Zimbabwe.

Section 8: Punishment for rape or certain none—consensual acts

1. Any person who, whether or not married to the person, without the consent of that person –

a. With the male organ, penetrates any part of the other person's body; or

b. With any object other that the male organ, penetrates the other person's genitalia or anus; or

c. Engage in fellatio or cunnilingus with the other person; shall be guilty of an offence and liable, subject to section sixteen, to the penalties

1. provided by law for rape. ee shall be sufficient for the purpose of paragraphs (a) and (b) of subsection (1).

Rape is an offence that depends on non-consent of the complainant. As such, for the court to convict on charges of rape, it should be proved that the victim did not consent to sexual intercourse. Chapter three of this book is vital.

In addition, marital rape is an offence in Zimbabwe. As a result it is rape for man to have sex with his wife without her consent. Furthermore, if it is a wife who has sex with her husband without his consent, she also commits rape. A fast sleeping person cannot consent to sexual intercourse. Hence, if a wife pushes her husband's organ into her body while he is sleeping, she commits rape. Equally, if husband has sex with a fast sleeping wife, he commits rape. He also commits rape if he uses any object, maybe a test tube, banana, bottle, etc. to penetrate his wife without her consent. A wife who uses an object to penetrate her husband's anus also commits rape. A wife or husband who engages in fellatio or cunnilingus acts without the consent of the other, commits an offence under section eight.

Any man who penetrates a woman with an object his organ without such woman's consent commits rape. A woman who has intercourse with a man without his consent, say he is sleeping, whether anal or vaginal intercourse, commits rape. A woman who pushes an object into a man's anus without his consent commits rape. A woman, who uses an object to penetrate another woman or girl without such person's consent, commits an offence.

Engaging in fellatio or cunnilingus acts with any person (whether male or female) without such person's consent amounts to an offence under section eight.

Section 16: Sentence for certain offences where offender is infected with HIV. Where a person is convicted of

a. rape or sodomy; or

b. having sexual intercourse with a young person in contravention of section three; or

c. having sexual intercourse with an intellectually handicapped person in contravention of section four; or

2. contravening subsection (1) of section eight by committing an act referred to in paragraph (a) or (c) of that subsection; and it is proved that, at the time of the offence, the convicted person was infected with HIV whether or not he was aware of his infection, he shall be sentenced to imprisonment for a period not exceeding twenty years.

If a person commits a sexual offence under Sections 3, 4 and 8 and he/she is found to be HIV positive the maximum sentence is 20 years imprisonment.

However, if his/her results are negative the maximum sentence for contravening Sections 3 and 4 is 10 years.

Sexual Offences In South Africa

South Africa has a draft Sexual Offences Bill (2003) to replace the outdated Sexual Offences Act 1957.

However, under the 1957Act, rape is when a male person has unlawful and intentional sexual intercourse with a female without her consent.

Unnatural forms of sexual intercourse like sodomy, bestiality are not offences in South Africa. The age of consent for homosexual activities is 19years and for heterosexuals is 16 years. The girls are protected under Section 14 of the Sexual Offences Act 1957, which states that unlawful carnal knowledge with a girl under the age of 16 years is an offence.

Sexual Offences In Nigeria

Nigeria, being a British Colony, the basis of its criminal law is English law. Nigeria has Northern Nigerian Penal Code and Criminal Code Act 1990.

However, by 1959, this law was not applicable to the people in the Northern region of Nigeria. As such, the Northern Nigerian Penal Code, was written to account for the differences between Muslim and non-Muslim laws. This made the country's criminal law applicable to all citizens.

The Northern Nigerian Penal Code is written to satisfy the Muslims as they are the majority in the Northern region. The guiding factor is that the Penal Code should not contradict the commands of the Holy Koran. Nigeria also uses Customary Law.

This law, like in Zambia, is based on the traditions of the people.

A. Criminal Code Act 1990 (Chapter 77 Laws of the Federation of Nigeria).

In Nigeria, according to the Criminal Code Act 1990, a male person under the age of twelve years is presumed to be incapable of having carnal knowledge. Under this Act, parties to offences or principal offenders, accessories after the fact and defences like intoxication and immature age are defined in the same way as in Zambia.

Also, the definition of unnatual offences, indecent treatment of boys under fourteen is the same as in Zambia.

Defilement

Section 218: Defilement of girls under thirteen

Any person who has unlawful carnal knowledge of a girl under the age of thirteen years is guilty of a felony, and is liable to imprisonment for life, with or without caning. Any person who attempts to have unlawful carnal knowledge of a girl under the age of thirteen years—is guilty of a felony, and is liable to imprisonment for fourteen years, with or without caning.

A prosecution for either of the offences defined in this section shall be begun within two months after the offence is committed. A person cannot be convicted of either of the offences defined in this section upon the uncorroborated testimony of one witness.

Section 221: Defilement of girls under sixteen and above thirteen, and of idiots. Any person who:-

1. has or attempts to have unlawful carnal knowledge of a girl being of or above thirteen years and under sixteen years of age; or

2. knowing a woman or girl to be an idiot or imbecile, has or attempts to have unlawful carnal knowledge of her; is guilty of a misdemeanour, and is liable to imprisonment for two years, with or without caning.

It is a defence to a charge of either of the offences firstly defined in this section to prove that the accused person believed, on reasonable grounds, that the girl was of or above the age of sixteen years.

A prosecution for any of the offences defined in this section shall be begun within two months after the offence is committed. A person cannot be convicted of any of the offences defined in this section upon the uncorroborated testimony of one witness.

222. Indecent treatment of girls under sixteen.

Any person who unlawfully and indecently deals with a girl under the age of sixteen years is guilty of a misdemeanour, and is liable to imprisonment for two years, with or without caning. If the girl is under the age of thirteen years, he is guilty of a felony and is liable to imprisonment for three years, with or without caning.

It is a defence to a charge the offence defined in this section to prove that the accused person believed, on reasonable grounds, that the girl was of or above the age of sixteen years.

The term "deal with " includes doing any act which, ifdone without consent, would constitute an assault, as hereinafter defined.

Section 222 of the Criminal Code Act 1990 discusses indecent assault.

Unlawful carnal knowledge

"Unlawful carnal knowledge" means carnal connection which takes place otherwise than between husband and wife. This means that according to the Criminal Code Act 1990, it is not unlawful for a man to be having sexual intercourse with a girl under 16 years as long as he is validly married to her. Chapter four is vital and Rex versus Chinjamba is an important case. However, since Section 218 offers a high penalty of life imprisonment, the idea of government is to over—protect girls less than 13 years. As such, the presumption should be that, marriage with a girl below 13 years is invalid.

Defilement of girls above 13 years but under 16 years attracts a two (2) years imprisonment. It is a defence to prove on reasonable grounds that the girl was above 16 years. The statutory defence is the same as in Zambia, as a result Chapter four is vital.

RAPE

The definition of rape is just like in Zambia word for word. As such, Chapter three of this book is vital to Nigerians.

357. Definition of rape

Any person who has unlawful carnal knowledge of a woman or girl, without her consent, or with her consent, if the consent is obtained by force or by means of threats or intimidation of any kind, or by fear of harm, or by means of false and fraudulent representation as to the nature of the act, or, in the case of a married woman, by personating her husband, is guilty of an offence which is called rape.

357. Punishment of rape

Any person who commits the offence of rape is liable to imprisonment for life, with or without caning.

357. Attempt to commit rape

Any person who attempts to commit the offence of rape is guilty of a felony, and is liable to imprisonment for fourteen years, with or without caning.

Indecent assault on females is defined in the same way like in Zambia, and so is attempt to commit rape and abduction of girls under sixteen.

B. The Northern Nigerian Penal Code

An example of the Northern Nigerian Penal Code is the Shari'ah Penal Code Law, 2000 enacted in Zamfara State of Nigeria. This Penal Code binds every person who professes the Islamic faith.

In this Penal Code, rape is defined in Chapter 8. Zina (Adultery or Fornication)

126. Zina defined

Whoever, being a man or a woman fully responsible, has sexual intercourse through the genital of a person over whom he has no sexual rights and in circumstances in which no doubt exists as to illegality of the act, is guilty of the offence of Zina.

127. Punishment for Zina

Whoever commits the offence of zina shall be punished:

a. with caning of one hundred lashes if unmarried, and shall also be liable to imprisonment for a term of one year; or

b. if married, with stoning to death (rajm).

EXPLANATION: Mere penetration is sufficient to constitute the sexual intercourse necessary to the offence of zina.

Rape

128. Rape defined

(1) A man is said to commit rape who, save in the case referred in subsection (2), has sexual intercourse with a woman in any of the following, circumstances:-

I. against her will; ii. without her consent, iii. with her consent, when her consent has been obtained by putting her in fear of death or of hurt;

with her consent, when the man knows that he is not her husband and that her consent is given because she believes that he is another man to whom she is or believes herself to be lawfully married; v. with or without her consent, when she is under fifteen years of age or of unsound mind.

(2) Sexual intercourse by a man with his own wife is not rape.

EXPLANATION: Mere penetration is sufficient to constitute the sexual intercourse necessary to the offence of rape.

Under Section 128(v), a girl below 15 years cannot consent to intercourse and if she does, then she is statutorily raped or defiled. Even if she is above 15 years but she is of unsound mind she is still raped. Just like in Zambia marital rape is not an offence among Muslims. Chapters three and four are relevant in Northern Nigeria.

129. Punishment for Rape

Whoever commits rape shall be punished: a. with caning of one hundred lashes if unmarried, and shall also be liable to imprisonment for a term of one year; or

b. if married with stoning to death c. in addition to either (a) or (b) above shall also pay the dowry of her equals

Sodomy is punishable with 100 lashes and one year imprisonment if not married and if married the accused person(s) shall be stoned to death.

Lesbianism and bestiality are punishable with 50 lashes and six months sentence. Incest

132. Incest defined

1. Whoever, being a man, has sexual intercourse with a woman who is and whom he knows or has reason to believe to be his daughter, his granddaughter, his mother or any other of his female ascendant or descendants, his sister or the daughter of his sister or brother or his paternal or maternal aunt has committed the offence of incest.

2. Whoever, being a woman, voluntarily permits a man who is and whom she knows or has reason to believe to be her son, her grandson her father or any other of her male ascendants or descendants, her brother or the son of her brother or sister or her paternal or maternal uncle to have sexual intercourse with her, has committed the offence of incest.

133. Punishment for Incest

Whoever commits incest shall be punished: a. with caning of one hundred lashes if unmarried, and shall also be liable to imprisonment for a term of one year; or

c. Engage in fellatio or cunniligus with the other person; shall be guilty of an offence and liable, subject to section sixteen, to the penalties provided by law for rape.

1. Penetration to any degree shall be sufficient for the purpose of paragraphs (a) and (b) of subsection (1).

Rape is an offence that depends on non-consent of the complainant. As such, for the court to convict on charges of rape, it should be proved that the victim did not consent to sexual intercourse. Chapter three of this book is therefore relevant to thing decision.

In addition, marital rape is an offence in Zimbabwe. As a result it is rape for man to have sex with his wife without her consent. Furthermore, if it is a wife who has sex with her husband without his consent, she also commits rape. A fast sleeping person cannot consent to sexual intercourse. Hence, if a wife pushes her husband's sexual organ into her body while he is sleeping, she commits rape.

Equally, if husband has sex with a fast sleeping wife, he commits rape. He also commits rape if he uses any object, be it a test tube, banana, bottle, etc. to penetrate his wife without her consent. A wife who uses an object to penetrate her husband's anus also commits rape. A wife

Summary, Suggestions and Conclusions

It is known fact that many people in the discussed countries have the capacity to combat sexual offences if only they are educated on how these offences are committed and the punishments thereafter. It can also be observed that the law on sexual offences is biased. Mostly, it favours females, when in fact males can also be victims. Unfortunately the same females are demanding for the castration of defilers and rapists. They believe that such a harsh punishment will deter others from abusing them.

The researcher of this piece is opposed to the demands of castration, as some men will end up being castrated for the offence they did not commit.

This could be the case as it is undoubtedly true that in homicides cases, all over the world, some convicts have been hanged until pronounced dead for the murder they did not commit.. Therefore, due to human error in identifying the suspect as well as failure by some law enforcement officers to do thorough investigations to determine the actual defiler or rapist, an innocent person may end up being castrated, going by the suggestion of the castration school of thought. A confession may only come after the castration, probably years later.

'Officers, I have now found out the man who attacked me at night and raped me nine months ago. The one you arrested is innocent.'

Meanwhile, the convict may have been castrated and lost power to have sex again. I presumed that the maximum life imprisonment punishment will be all right as at now.

If there is anything Parliament can do urgently, it is to include indecent exposure as a criminal offence, so that prostitutes parading the streets at night can be arrested for indecent exposure. Indecent exposure definitely has a bearing on rape, defilement and incest. The duty of Parliament is to enact good laws so that citizens are protected from any form of criminal activities, and most Penal

Codes, have several serious weaknesses that make the law enforcement fail to do their job properly.

How to Deal with Sex Offenders

I propose a law be passed that requires all sex offenders, to register, and wear a tracking device. By wearing such a device, the police would have a better way or chance of identifying them.

That the safety of our children is of the utmost importance is not in question. Just like the 1994 Jacob Wetterling Act requires that persons convicted of sex crimes against children register with state authorities, this type of legislation is necessary because the prison system in Zambia is already overcrowded. It would not be possible to lock up sex offenders and throw away the key, even though this is what many Zambians would be happier to see done. So we have registration laws. These laws are evidence that the people want more tools available to law enforcement to find sex offenders who may be responsible for missing children.

There should be access to the information on the internet to enables parents find out where and how many sex offenders are in their area. This information should be available because it is widely believed that sex offenders pose a high risk of re-offending after release from custody.

Even without public access, registration of child sex offenders is still a valuable tool to law enforcement officials. Although it is a valuable tool, it is not enough. When a registered sex offender changes residence, it is up to the individual to notify the authorities of his change of address. Here in lies a fundamental flaw in the system as we cannot accept that the safety of our children be dependent on the "honour " of a convicted criminal. We cannot trust a sex offender to notify the authorities every time he/she moves. A tracking device would make certain that we know where he/she is.

I suggest that the Zambia government should lead in Africa the implementation of required law a brand new legislation under this law, persons convicted of sexually motivated crimes on children under the age of twelve, will be faced with 25 years minimum to life confinement. Also, if released from prison, they will have to wear a tracking device for the rest of their lives. This is more than I am asking for, but is certainly acceptable.

Global Positioning System (G.P.S) is a relatively new technology that uses satellites to locate a device. This technology has been used by the military, automobile manufacturers, and others. GPS, used in automobiles for tracking by the owners in case theft, among other uses, is one known application of the technology. By placing a G.P.S. tracking device on sex offenders, law enforcement officials will be able to locate them to within 15 Metres radius of his actual location. The program will also have the capability to record movements of the individual so that if a crime occurs, officials will be able to tell if a sex offender was at the scene. The tracking system will also alert officials if a sex offender enters restricted zones such as schools and playgrounds or a specific address specified under the offenders terms of release.

I believe that placing a tracking device on convicted sex offenders would greatly reduce the number of repeat offences because people are less likely to commit a crime if they believe that they will be caught. Tracking should be an excellent deterrent.

One problem with the device however is that it can be removed by the person wearing it. However, if such an act occurs, a warning would be sent to authorities who could then try to locate him by starting from his last known position. This problem, however, may be fixed in the future through technology which might permit an implanted device.

Evidence that the people want this system can be found in a survey that I conducted. It shows that the public does not believe that the government of Zambia is doing enough to protect our nations' children, 95 percent to be exact. While 38 percent of those polled think that a tracking device on convicted sex offenders would be a violation of their individual rights, an overwhelming 81 percent think that they should be required to wear them anyway (survey). With numbers like these, it seems apparent that tracking devices will become commonplace on convicted sex offenders. Options to the tracking program should be legislated in Zambia. One such option has been in effect elsewhere? In Southern Africa. In this legislation, sex offenders deemed high risk, must identify themselves to neighbours and local residents. This law has run into a mess of legal challenges. The sex offenders are claiming an infringement of their rights (Hanson Perverts).

In summary, I believe that I have shown ample evidence that my plan, in addition to being cost effective, and what the people want, will deter sex offenders from repeat offences.

When a woman commits a sexual offence, what should we do? Sexual offence committed by a female is as disgusting, repulsive and horrible as when committed by a man. When children are victims of sexual offence, it is the worst possible crime, because they cannot defend themselves. Female sex offenders should be prosecuted to the full extent of the law and programs should be made to monitor and rehabilitate them.

What should we do when a woman commits a sexual offence? The punishment should be determined by the gravity of the nature of sexual offenses committed. Woman who commit rape, sodomy or abuse with an object, against anyone, should go to jail. If the woman committed these crimes against a child (0-18), the sentence for this crime should be for life, without the chance of parole. If the same crime is committed against an adult, the jail sentence should be 25 years to life.

Sexual Harassment Interventions

Sexual harassment affects people of all ages and races and of both sexes. Evidence of this is apparent in the increased number of grievances filed with the Zambia Equal Employment Opportunity Commission (EEOC): from 10,532 filings in 1993 to 15,889 in 1997 (Ganzel 1998). The Court rulings in Suspect v. City of Boca Raton and Burlington Industries v. Ellerth are an attempt to halt these incidents by requiring harassed employees to work within their companies to resolve grievances before turning to the EEOC. They place responsibility on the employer to set guidelines for preventing sexual harassment and on the employee to follow them (Barrier 1998).

What Institutions Can Do

Emerging from the literature on sexual harassment and prevention are three key steps that employers can take to counter sexual harassment (Kimble-Ellis 1998; "Protecting Employees" 1998):

1. Develop a strong company policy that specifies in writing outlawed behaviours and penalties for their demonstration

2. Establish grievance procedures for reporting; processing, and resolving complaints

3. Provide sexual harassment training for supervisors, managers, and workers that explains what sexual harassment means and how it can be recognized, confronted, and averted.

Strong Company Policy

Although a number of large companies have already established policies governing sexual harassment, effective compliance with the law on sexual harassment requires that all companies, as well as schools that receive federal funds, establish sexual harassment policies that they put in writing, disseminate, and enforce (Barrier 1998).Acompany policy addressing sexual harassment must clearly specify;

(1) the behaviours that constitute harassment and the company's intolerance of such behaviours;

(2) channels employees must follow to report sexual harassment complaints to their s u p e r v i s o r s o r d e s i g n a t e d c o m p a n y representative;

(3) strategies the company will follow in investigating and resolving a complaint, including confidentiality practices;

(4) Warnings that violation of the policy will result in punishments that could include dismissal; and

(5) assurance that retaliation will not be allowed (Ganzel 1998).

Good policy statements reflect collaboration among executives, supervisors, and employees and among administrators, teachers, and students. They respond to the organizational climate, which includes family and community as well as school influences. Because "sexual harassment is a manifestation of deeply held beliefs, attitudes, feelings, and cultural norms . ., it is predicated on sociocultural views and sex-role stereotypes" (Brandenburg 1997, p. 39). It reflects the abuse of power, a gender—power differential; and sometimes power—related retaliation. Some authors add sexual orientation power struggles to that list (ibid.).

In an address to educators at a conference organized by the Safe School Coalition, Marjorie Fink, a national sexual harassment prevention trainer, identified climate as a major component to guide prevention efforts ("Trainer: Stop Bullying"1999). Every school, like every business, has its unique climate. In some organizations, verbal teasing, dirty jokes, and sexual pictures may be the d o m i n a n t b e h a v i o u r t h a t r e f l e c t s s e x u a l harassment; in others, improper touching, stalking, or shoving may be the misbehaviour (ibid.). When all members of a work organization or school become involved in establishing policy, these contextual issues can be more effectively addressed and behaviours targeted.

Grievance Procedures

Although companies are required by law to handle grievances internally before seeking outside litigation, schools are also finding internal grievances procedures to be more effective in handling sexual harassment complaints. "Internal grievance procedures may save time, minimize emotional and financial expense, and be more sensitive to all persons" (Brandenburg 1997, p. 53). Effective grievance procedures should clearly define the steps for submitting complaints, both informally and formally. Procedures for informal complaints should detail how the harassed person should go about seeking advice or counsel about a proper response to the offending behaviour and describe the process of mediation, negotiation, and problem solving that may be used to resolve the issue. Procedures for formal complaints should require that the grievance be submitted in writing and present all facts related to the incident—who, what, where, when, the scope of the incident, and names of individuals involved. Typically, these reports must be submitted immediately after the incident, not weeks later. However, it is the responsibility of each company and school tospecify the procedures it wants its employees or students to follow.

Grievance procedures should also identify the person or persons to whom grievances must be submitted. In the grievance officer model, all complaints are processed through a designated supervisor or officer; in the grievance board or committee model, grievances are submitted to a group (Brandenburg 1997).Although the grievance officer model offers the advantage of one entry point for complaint submission, it has the disadvantage of possibly requiring the harassed employee to deal with someone with whom he or she may be uncomfortable. The committee model, which places the problem in the hands of many, has t h e d i s a d v a n t a g e o f r e q u i r i n g g r e a t e r communication and coordination between committee members and the harassed employee, making it more difficult to ensure confidentiality (ibid.).

Whatever process is adopted, the procedures the grievance officer/committee will follow must also be identified, e.g., receive the written complaint, identify the specific harassment, interview complainants, interview the accused, interview witnesses, determine if sexual harassment has occurred, present the findings to both parties along with the consequences of the action, and require employees to accept mandatory arbitration ("Protecting Employees" 1998).

Sexual Harassment Prevention Training

No policy or set of grievance procedures will be effective unless all employees, from supervisors to line workers, administrators to custodial staff, are knowledgeable about the company's policy and grievance procedures.

To prevent vulnerability to sexual harassment allegations, an organization must provide access to training for all employees and document their participation in and completion of the training program. Employees need to be aware that, although the law held companies liable for h a r a s s m e n t b y s u p e r v i s o r s e v e n w h e n management was unaware of the incidents, they made it clear that companies cannot be held liable for incidents in which an harassed employee did not follow the company's reporting procedures or did not participate in company-sponsored sexual harassment prevention training ("Protecting Employees" 1998).

Sexual harassment training should explain the law that prohibits sexual harassment, identify the actions that may be categorized as sexual harassment, describe the company's policy and its grievance procedures.

However, the training should also heighten awareness of sexual harassment and present strategies for intervention.

Effective programs define sexual harassment and provide information on its incidence. Sexual harassment should be defined as "unwanted sexual attention that would be offensive to a reasonable person and that negatively affects the work or school environment" (Brandenburg 1997, p. 1). The key word in the definition is "unwanted." Two categories of sexual harassment may be given to guide thinking during the training program: quid pro quo harassment and hostile environment harassment. Quidproquo harassment occurs "w h e n submission to or rejection of such (unwelcome sexual) conduct by an individual is used as the basis for employment decisions affecting such individual" (ibid., p. 2). Hostile environment harassment, on the other hand, occurs "when unwelcome sexual conduct causes the environment to become hostile, intimidating, or offensive, and unreasonably interferes with an employee's or student's work" (ibid., p. 3). Training programs should ensure that participants understand these definitions so that they can construct their own meanings of sexual harassment as they discuss the experiences of others.

Effective programs reflect good teaching and learning practices. They are descriptive, intensive, relevant, and positive (Berkowitz 1998):

They require the involvement of all members of a company or school and include family and community members who have an influence on the employees' or students' life.

They offer participatory, problem-based learning experiences that are interactive and actively engage the student in learning.

They are tailored to the "age, community culture, and socioeconomic status of the trainee and are contextualized to the individual's peer group experiences" (ibid., p. 3).

They present information from a positive viewpoint, encouraging healthy behaviour rather than forbidding poor behaviour.

Effective programs teach intervention skills. Berkowitz (1998) identifies the following steps for converting bystander behaviour to intervention (pp. 3-4):

Help learners to recognize sexual harassment incidents by providing them with appropriate and relevant definitions and examples of sexual harassment.

Sexual harassment training programs for a business or school organization's supervisors and employees can be internally or externally provided.

Although the sources of training may vary across organizations, each program should result in the achievement of designated learning outcomes. Case studies, scenarios, and ill-structured problems offer ways to connect knowledge about sexual harassment to its prevention in the workplace. The ultimate success of a company's or school's sexual harassment prevention training program will be reflected in the organization's ability to eliminate the behaviour and avoid sexual harassment lawsuits.

APPENDIX

Extracts from the Penal Code

(Amendment) Bill 2005
[The bill is almost an Act as it has passed third reading and only awaiting presidential assent] Zambia has amended the penal code in order to domesticate in the part, the Convention on the Rights of the Child and to provide stiffer penalties in respect of sexual offences committed against children and other person so as to deter offenders from committing such crimes.

The Act shall be read as one with the main penal code. Section 131A: Definition of a child In this part "child" mean a person below the age of sixteen years

Section 138: Defilement of child

1. Any person who unlawfully and carnally knows any child commits a felony and is liable, upon conviction, to a term of imprisonment of not less than fifteen years and may be liable to imprisonment for life.

2. And person who attempt to have unlawful carnal knowledge of any child commit a felony and is liable, upon conviction, to imprisonment for a term not less than fourteen years and not exceeding twenty years.

3. Any person who prescribes the defilement of a child as a cure for an ailment commits a felony and is liable, upon conviction, to imprisonment

for a term of not less than f i f t e e n ye a r s a n d m a y b e l i a b l e t o imprisonment for life.

4. A child above the age of twelve years who commits an offence under subsection (1) and (2) is liable, to such community service or counseling as the court may determine, in the best interests of both children.

There isn't much difference between the old section 138 and the new section 138. However, defilement now will be applicable to both boys and girls under 16 years of age. The new law introduces minimum sentence of 15 years for defilement and 14 years for an attempt. It also introduces community sentencing and counseling for offenders aged between 12 and 16 years. Additionally, the statutory defense has been removed.

Analysis of the New Section 138

1. Mandatory HIV test for defilers

This law does not include mandatory HIV test for defilers to determine whether the defiler is HIV positive or not. Zambians have cried that most defilers sleep with children so that they can get cured of HIV/AIDS. Of course, it is difficult to explain why a grown up man, say 40 years old, would have sex with a 2-year –old baby girl. As such, Parliament should have included a mandatory HIV test for defilers so that those found HIV test for defilers so that those found HIV positive are given a harsh sentence. As indicated on pages 126-128 of this book, it is evident that girls are defiled and given the deadly virus.

Probably, the failure to include such a requirement has to do with Human Rights principle. However, it must be noted that Children do have right as well. And, whoever does not respect the right of other should not expect his/her right to be respected. One cannot claim for equality when he does not treat other with equity, for as the maximum goes that he who comes to equity must have clean hands.

Zambia could not have been the first country to include HIV testing in the penal code for sexual offenders: Botswana and Zimbabwe have already done it.

2. Minimum sentence of 15 years Defilement of under 16's, girls and boys aged between one day and 14 year is unpardonable and perpetrators should be given harsh sentence to show the gravity of the offence, to emphasize public disapproval, to punish the offenders and above all, to protect the children. However, let it not forgotten that defilement extends to girls (and boys) ages between 14 and 16 years . As such, sentencing should be based on age of the offender as well as age of the victim and the manner in which the defilement was committed. Mitigation is also a guiding factor when sentencing. Minimum sentence is explained on page 108 and 112 It is evident that some girls between 14 and 16 are having petty relationship with their teenage boyfriend and the majority of these are having sex.

It is upon considering the age of the offender, the age of the victim, the manner in which the offender was committed and the mitigation of the accused that a minimum sentence of five years for defilement of girls ages below 14 and one year for defilement of girls aged between 14 and 16 was proposed on page 110. The guiding factor to such minimum sentence being a formula : P+ (16-N) + XAs indicated on page 110 N is dependent upon the age of the victim and X is any additional period which must be greater than or equal to zero. X depends upon the age of the offender, manner in which the offence was committed and mitigation of the offender.

As such if a 40-years-old man has sex with 151/2—year-old girl with her consent, he should be given a harsh sentence because at 40, he must be wise and should not have lustful sexual passion for girls. On the other hand if any 18 1/2 –year-old young man has intercourse with a 15-years-old girl with her consent and because she is pregnant he is arrested for defilement, he should be given a lenient sentence. Sentence makes him appreciate that sex with girls under 16 is an offence. The purpose of sentencing him is to rehabilitate and reform him so that after serving his sentence he can be useful to the nation and be able to contribute to national development. If he is given a lenient sentence of 2 1/2years imprisonment, at 21, when he come out of prison, he is still energetic to be able to go to college or university and study. Supposing he finally graduates as a medical doctor, the country will have simply succeeded in turning a criminal into a medical doctor who will save the lives of many people and be able to support a family. That is how a nation develops. It is by turning worthless youths into useful ones. The question for members of the public is: Is 15 years minimum sentence a lenient sentence for a youth aged 18 1/2, if sentence to 15 years imprisonment, he can only be free when he is 33 1/2years old. At that age, can he go to college or university? Can he remember the mathematics, biology, chemistry, principles of accounts that he learnt at secondary school even if he passed his grade 12 exams with excellent results? What rehabilitation and reformation has the nation done to him? Are prisons now training centres where a prisoner can get a diploma or degree? Such a man will have no hope of a better future and whilst in prison. He will have learnt all the bad ways of life and upon being released from prison, he is likely to be a robber, or worse criminal than he was. Besides, because of long stay in prison, he would have adapted to prison condition such that going back for another offence would not make him apprehensive. In short a harsh minimum sentence will turn many youth into useless citizens.

Supposing the defiled 15 1/2—years –old girl was in grade 11, consented to sex with the 18 1/2-years-old youth because she believed she was in love and assuming the young man was HIV negative, in 15 years' time, what can she possible do? Can she go back to school after giving birth, to finish grade 12 and go to university? Defilement was put at 16 year in 1941. From 1941 to date, haven't society seen some women who made mistake of getting pregnant whilst at school go back to school and later on enter university and now are respected people in society? If yes than when her defiler, the man she loved, come out of prison, he will find her either working as an. Accountant or a lawyer or a doctor, etc.

It should be known that all youths using force (whether physical or constructive) when defiling girls (or boy) don't deserve leniency but should be given harsh sentences because forced sex is painful not only physically but also mentally. As such, a harsh sentence can keep such a youth from

202

society for a long time. The idea is to severely punish him because the manner in which the offence was committed was bad, so that as the girl is going through the trauma of sexual abuse he is also suffering in prison. However, making a minimum sentence of 15 years applicable to every defiler regardless of the manner in which an offence was committed, age of the victim and mitigation, is not right.

Parliament should have considered section 7 of the criminal procedure code, which, as indicated on page 129, guides magistrates as to the maximum sentence they can give.

The SRM and PRM, who can sentence up to nine years, are only found in provincial headquarters and big districts, like Kitwe. As a result, 15 years minimum sentence means that all defilement cases will be (tried and) sentenced by high court judges. This means that such cases will have to be transferred to provincial headquarters.

It is also to be noted that, not all provinces have resident judges, but circuit judges go to these provinces. Consequently, I defilement occurs in Kaputa or Nakonde, the case has to be committed to kasama High court. Ajudge will have to come from Ndola after sometime. Then, how long will it take for the victim to get justice? In reality, there will be more delay in case disposal. This will increase corruption and withdrawal of cases. There will also be an increase in concealment of defilement as it is true that in a community, every person belongs to that society, and harmony is promoted than disharmony. Subsequently, parent or relatives to the offender will be kneeling before the victim's family and offering a lot of money in order to be forgiven in addition, our traditions dictate that a girl is a lady ready for marriage after reaching puberty, and so chances are that if a girl has reached puberty, parent would rather receive and get her married money than have the offender prosecuted.

Section 138(2) discusses attempted defilement. Considering the above information on minimum sentence, a 14 years minimum sentence for an attempt is too harsh.

Section 138(3) reads; "Any person who prescribes the defilement of a child as a cure for an ailment commits a felony and. . . ."According to the Oxford Advanced Learners Dictionary, an ailment is an illness that is not very serious. Section 138(3) is simply talking about counselors and procurers. For example, a traditional doctor who prescribes that for a man to become rich or be cured of HIV, he needs to have intercourse with a young virgin of less than 16 years, is a counselor who has planned how defilement will occur. Is HIV a non—serious illness? Anyway, counselors or procurers or abettor, are dealt with under section 21 of the principal penal code. As a result section 138(3) is repetition of the law.

Section 138(4) reads; "A child above the age of 12 years who commit an offence under Subsection (1) and (2) is liable, to such community service or counseling . . . . . ."

Section 14(3) of penal is explained on page 54 and 55 and it talks about the presumption that a boy under 12 years is incapable of having sexual intercourse. However, section 138(4) goes a step further by indicating that a child between 12 and 16 years if he commits a sexual offence he should be given a community service (sentence) or should undergo counseling. In defilement, consent of a girl who has consented to intercourse, Section 138 (4) is justified and he can undergo counseling or be given a community service. Suppose at 15 ½, he has intercourse with another 13 year old girl, this time impregnating her, should he be given a community sentence or undergo counseling again? Suppose he uses physical force to penetrate a 12 year old girl who has just become of age, hence taking away her precious virginity, should he be given a community sentence? Definitely counseling is out, for she did not consent.

Section 138(4) has a weakness. It should have read as follows. " . . . to such imprisonment or community service or counseling as the court may determine, in the best interest of both children." As such, such a child offender can be sent to a reformatory school.

3. Removal of the Statutory Defence.

The proviso contained in the previous Section 138 as indicated on page 42 and explained in detail from pages 61 to 64 is very vital to case of defilement.

In chapter two, it is indicated that in every crime, the actus reus and mens rea have to be proved. In statutory rape, actus reus is the causation of the crime and is described as the conduct of having intercourse with a girl under 16 years. Mens rea is the guilty state of the mind and is described as knowledge by a man (or woman) that a girl (or boy) is under 16years or recklessness as to whether or not a girl is below 16 An accused person will be deemed to have had knowledge of the age of the victim if: (a) He is a close neighbour to the girl. (b) He stays in the same neighbourhood with the girl and he has seen her grow, and many have even attended her birthday parties before. (c). He was familiar with the victim despite the fact that they don't stay in the same neighbourhood.

(d).Athird party told him that the girl was below 16 years. (e). the girl told him about her age or he had statistical information about her age. For example, a teacher can check from the pupils' file for the girl's age.

It is in this regard that previously, for an accused to be convicted, the prosecution had to allege that he had knowledge that a girl was below 16 years and it was up to him to prove that he had reasonable cause to believe that the girl was above 16 years and he had reasonable grounds to in fact hold this belief. If the accused says he had no knowledge of the girl's age, then the prosecution would say he was reckless or very careless such that he did not bother to find out about the girl's age. As such, he would be convicted.

The idea behind the provison was to make a man liable who had reasonable cause to believed so. Otherwise, the statutory defence would not work for him.

A belief that a girl was over 16 cannot be held to be reasonable if it is based on imagination. It can only be reasonable if it is based on facts or good reasons. For example, if trial commences within a short period of time after the occurrence of defilement, say two months, the court was obliged to look at the girl's appearance if the accused said she told him that she was over 16 years of age. However, it was difficult to consider such a defence after a long period of time. The proviso offered limited help to the accused. But in few cases, it helped the accused.

As the new law stands, the accused person has no defence to rely upon. Even if he had good reasonable grounds to prove before the court that the girl was above 16, he cannot advance those reasons. The current law does not allow him to do so. Chapter nine of this book proves that the proviso is useful. Zambia is the first country in the region to do away with the statutory defence. The reasoning behind its removal being that defilers were relying too much on it, as such, some ended being acquitted. The truth is that the proviso was being abused not only by the defiler but also the party who did not bother to verify the assertions of the accused. An accused person can say anything in defence but if what he says is accepted without serious consideration of the law by the magistrate and the prosecution, then the blame cannot be put on him or the law.

Every crime has a defence. Even murder has defences.

For example, if malice aforethought cannot be proved, the offence is reduced to manslaughter.

Other defences are provocation and killing of a person in protection of life and property.

Accordingly, it is just fair that defilement also has a defence.

Section 137: Indecent Assault

1. Any person who unlawfully and indecently assaults any child or other person commits a felony and is liable, upon conviction, to imprisonment for term not less than fifteen years and not exceeding 20 years.

2. It shall not be a defence to a charge of an indecent assault on a child to prove that the child consented to the act of indecency.

3. Any person who is found in any building or dwelling house or in any veranda or passage attached thereto or in any yard, garden or other land

adjacent to or dwelling house or in any veranda or passage attached thereto or in any yard, garden or other land adjacent to or within the cartilage of such building or dwelling – house not being a public place –

a. For the purpose of and from motives of indecent curiosity gazing at or observing any other person or child who may be therein while in a state of undress or semi-undressed; or b. With intent to annoy or indecently to assault any child or other person who may be therein; commits and offence and is liable, upon conviction, to imprisonment for a term not less than two years and not exceeding five years.

The new law is beneficial as men can now complain for indecent assault as there are women who like raping men or indecently assaulting them. Apart from the fact that now men can be indecently assaulted, there are no major changes in the law. Of course minimum sentence of 15 years is considered too hash. Section 139: Defilement of imbecile or Person with Mental Illness

Any person who knowing a child or other person to be an imbecile or person with a mental illness, has or attempt to have unlawful carnal knowledge of that child or other person in circumstances not amounting to rape, but which proves that the offender knew at the time of the commission of the offence that the child or other person was an idiot or imbecile commits a felony and is liable, upon conviction, to imprison for a term of not less than 14 years and may be liable to imprisonment for life.

Defilement of an imbecile or a person with mental illness is explained on page 32 under title: "Consent of a person of unsound mind."

Section 159-161: Incest

The minimum sentence for incest is 20 years. Incest is now extended to adoptive brother and adoptive sister. This contradicts the universal principle among former British colonies that incest is an offence of blood relationship.

Other Offences of Public Importance Section 137A: Sexual Harassment

1. Any person who practices sexual harassment in a workplace, institution of learning or elsewhere on a child commits a felony and is liable, upon conviction, to imprisonment for a term not less than three years and not exceeding 15 years.

2. A child who commits an offence under subsection (1) is liable to such community service or counselling as the court may determine in the best interest of the child.

3. In this Section, sexual harassment means-

a. A seductive sexual advance being unsolicited sexual comment, physical contact or other gesture of a sexual nature which finds objectionable or offensive or which causes discomfort in one's studies or job and interferes with academic performance or a conducive working or study environment;

b. Sexual bribery in the form of soliciting or attempting to solicit sexual activity by promise or reward;

c. Sexual threat or coercion which includes procuring or attempting to procure sexual activity by threat of violence or victimization; or

d. Sexual imposition using forceful behaviour or assault in an attempt to gain physical sexual contact.

Section 143: Selling or Trafficking in Children, Etc. Any person who sells or traffics in a child or other person for any purpose or in any form commits an offence and is liable, upon conviction, to imprisonment for a term of not less than 20 years.

Provided that where it is proved during the trial of the accused person that the sale or trafficking in a child or other person was for the purpose of causing that child or person to be unlawfully and carnally known by another person, whether such carnal knowledge was intended to be with any particular person or generally, the person is liable, upon conviction, to imprisonment for life.

Section 177: Child Pornography

1. Any person who engages a child or other person a. In a pornographic performance b. In the production of pornographic film or other material; or c. In a pornographic activity of any nature commits an offence an is liable, upon conviction, to a term of imprisonment of not less than 15years and may be liable to imprisonment for life.

1. Any person who –

a. Sells to a child pornographic material;

b. Compels a child to watch a pornographic film or view pornography on the internet or elsewhere or in any form intended to corrupt a child's morals; commit an offence and is liable, upon conviction, to a term of imprisonment of not less than 15 years.

1. A child who commits an offence under Subsection (2) is liable, to such community service or counselling as the court may determine in the best interest of the child.

Section 168: Desertion of Child

Any person who being the parent, guardian or other person having the lawful care or charge of a child being able to maintain such child, willfully and without lawful or reasonable cause desert the child and leaves it without means of support commits an offence and is liable, upon conviction, for a first offence to imprisonment for a term not exceeding three years, or for a subsequent offence for a term not exceeding seven years.

Section 169: Neglecting to Provide Food etc. for Children

Any person who being-

a. Parent; (b) Guardian; or (c) person in charge; of a child that is unable to provide for itself, refuses or willfully neglects to provide, being able to do so, sufficient food, clothes, bedding or other necessities for such child and thereby injures the health of such child, commits an offence and is liable, on conviction, to a fine not exceeding one hundred thousand penalty units or imprisonment for a term not exceeding three years or to both.

BIBLIOGRAPHY

Bakan, J. 1997. Just Words: Constitutional Rights and Social Wrongs. Toronto: University of Toronto Press.

Bauman, Z. 1991. Modernity and Ambivalence. Cambridge: Polity Press. – 1993. Postmodern Ethics. Oxford: Blackwell. Blackstone 4 Comm 64-65.

Barrier, M. "Sexual Harassment." Nation's Business 86, no. 12 (December 1998): 14-19.

Berkowitz, A. D. "How We Can Prevent Sexual Harassment and SexualAssault." Educator's Guide to Controlling Sexual Harassment 6, no. 1 (October 1998): 1—4.

Brandenburg, J.B. Confronting Sexual Harassment. New York: Teacher's College, Columbia University, 1997. Comack, E. 1999. Locating Law: Class, Race & Gender.

Halifax: Fernwood Publishing. Condon, M. 1998. Making Disclosure: Ideas and Interests in Ontario Securities Regulation. Toronto: University of Toronto Press.

Crosby, A. 1997. The Measure of Reality: Quantification and Western Society, 1250-1600. Cambridge: Cambridge University Press.

Criminal Code (NT) s 155, considered by Kearney J in Rv Salmon (1994) 70ACrim R536 Edwin M. Borchard, professor of law in Yale University:

Convicting the Innocent, errors of criminal justice,Archon Book (Hamden Connection) – 1961. Foucault, M. 1977. Discipline and Punish: The Birth of the Prison. New York: Pantheon Books.

1980. Power/Knowledge: Selected Interviews and Other Writings. Edited by Colin Gordon. New York: Pantheon Books.

1990. History of Sexuality. New York: Vintage Books. FrancisAdams, Hons Sir: *Criminal law and practice in New Zealand;* Sweet and Maxwell Ltd. – 1964.

Fudge, J., and B. Cossman. 2002. "Introduction: Privatization, Law and the Challenge to Feminism." In Privatization, Law and the Challenge to Feminism, 3-40. Toronto: University of Toronto Press. Ganzel, R. "What Sexual- Harassment Training Really Prevents. "Training" 35, no. 10 (October 1998): 86-94.

Garland, D. 1999. "Governmentality and the Problem of Crime." In Governable Places, edited by R. Smandych, 15-44.Aldershot, UK: Ashgate/

Dartmouth. Glanville Williams: Criminal Law 2nd edition; Stephen and Sons Ltd – 1961. H. C. Underhill (of the New York bar): Underhill's

Criminal Evidence Part 3; the Bobbs-Merrill Company Inc. Publishers 1957.

Haggerty, K. 2001. Making Crime Count. Toronto: University of Toronto Press.

Hunt, A. 1996. "The Governance of Consumption: Sumptuary Laws and Shifting Forms of Regulation." Economy and Society 25: 410-27. John Smith, Sir, (and the late Brian Hogan):

Criminal Law 8th edition; Butterworths – 1986 Books. 1990. History of Sexuality. New York: Vintage

Kimble-Ellis, S. "Safeguard against Sexual Harassment." Black Enterprise 29, no. 5 (December 1998): 36.

Krajnc,A. 2000. "Wither Ontario's Environment? Neo—Conservatism and the Decline of the Environment Ministry." Canadian Public Policy, March.

Mason A, 'Law and Morality' (1995) 4 Griffith LR 147. MansourAA, 'Hudud Crimes' in the Islamic Criminal Justice System (1982) p 199

Morrison, W. 1995. Theoretical Criminology: From Modernity to Post— Modernism. London Cavendish.

Pennington, H. 2000. "Recent Experiences in Food Poisoning." In Food, Science, Policy and Regulation in the Twentieth Century, edited by D. Smith and J. Phillips, 223-38. London: Routledge.

Pennington Group. 2000. Report on the circumstances leading to the 1996 Outbreak of Infection with E. coli 0157 in Central Scotland. Edinburgh, Stationery Office.

Philipps, L. 1996. "Discursive Deficits: A Feminist Perspective on the Power of Technical Knowledge in Fiscal Law and Policy." Canadian Journal of Law and Society 11, 1: 141-76.

Puri, P. 2001. "Sentencing the Criminal Corporation." Osgoode Hall Law Journal 39, 2/3 (Summer/Fall): 612-53.

"Protecting Employees-and Your Business." Nation's Business 86, no. 12 (December 1998): 18-19.

Snider, L. 1999. "Relocating Law: Making Corporate Crime Disappear." In Locating Law: Race/ Class/Gender Connections, edited by E. Comack, 183—206. Halifax: Fernwood Publishing. 2000. "The Sociology of Corporate Crime: An Obituary." Theoretical Criminology 4, 2:169-205.

2001a. "Abusing Corporate Power: Death of a Concept." In (Ab)Using Power: The Canadian Experience, edited by S. Boyd, D. Chunn, and R. Menzies, 112-30. Halifax: Fernwood Publishing.

2001b. "Feminist Political Economy and Law." Paper presented at the conference Feminist Political Economy and the Law: Revitalizing the Debate. Institute for Feminist Legal Studies, Osgoode Hall Law School, 24 March.

P.M.A. Hunt: South African Criminal Law and Procedure;Juta and Co., Limited-1970.

Tombs, S. 1992. "Stemming the Flow of Blood? The Illusion of Self-Regulation." Journal of Human Justice: Special Issue on Corporate Crime 3, 2: 1-18.

1996. "Injury, Death and the Deregulation Fetish: The Politics of Occupational Safety Regulation in United Kingdom Manufacturing Industries." International Journal of Health Services 26, 2: 309- 29.

1999. "Death and Work in Britain," The Sociological Review 47, 2: 345-67. – And D. Whyte.

2004. "Scrutinizing the Powerful? Crime, Contemporary Political Economy and Critical Social Research." In Researching the Powerful edited by S. Tombs and D. Whyte. London: Peter Lang. 184 Laureen Snider Ronald A. Anderson: Whaton's Criminal Law and Procedure Part 1; The Lawyers Co-orperative Publishing Company of New York – 1957.

Tucker, E. 1995. "And Defeat Goes On: An Assessment of 'Third-Wave' Health and Safety Regulation."

In Corporate Crime: Contemporary Debates, edited by F. Pearce and L. Snider, 245-67. Toronto: University of Toronto Press. Utah CodeAnn 76-7-103.

"Sexual Harassment Training Online." Best's Review 99, no. 9 (January 1999): 82.

"Trainer: Stop Bullying and Teasing in K-6 to Prevent Sexual Harassment Now, Later. " Educator's Guide to Controlling Sexual Harassment: Monthly Bulletin 6, no. 4 (January 1999): 1, 3.

Walkerton Inquiry. 2002. Report of the Walkerton Inquiry. Part 1. The Events of May 2000 and Related Issues. Dennis R. O' [commissioner]. Toronto: Ontario Ministry of the Attorney-General.

Wayne R. LaFave: Arrest: the decision to take a suspect into custody; Little Brown and Co. – 1965. Weinstein JD, 'Adultery Law and the State: A History' (1987) 38 Hastings LJ 195 at 225.

GLOSSARY

~ (This glossary is vital only for the purpose of this book) Abrasion: a scratch; a damaged area of the skin where it has been rubbed by something hard.

Acquit: set free; to decide and state officially in court of law that somebody is not guilty of a crime he was charged with.

Act: doing something by somebody. In criminal law and act has to do with conduct-offences. Conduct—offences are 'doing offences' like murder, rape incest, defilement, etc. see omission.

Aggravated Robbery: stealing (from a person, house, bank, etc.) using weapons (e.g. knives, guns, etc.)

Aider: a person who helps or assists another during the commission of the crime.

Amending: to change a law slightly in order to correct a mistake Appellant: a person who asks a higher court to consider a decision made by the lower court of law

Assailant: a person who attacks somebody, especially physically

Assertion: declaration; Statement saying that you strongly believe something is true

Assumption: best guess; a belief that something is true although there is no proof

Binding case or precedent: a court's decision that is decided in Zambia, Northern Rhodesia or a commonwealth country, which the court needs to follow. A lower or equivalent court is always bound by the decision in that case until it is overruled by the Supreme Court (see persuasive case)

Blackmail: the crime of demanding something (money) from a person by threatening to tell somebody else a secret about them Carnal knowledge: sexual intercourse Catalyst: a person or thing that causes a change (e.g. in making decision) Charge: official claim by the police that somebody has committed an offence

Chronological: sequential; order in which things should happen Common wealth: an organization that is part of the United Kingdom and most of the countries that used to be part of the British Empire.

Compliant: Accuser; a person who reports a person who has committed an offence to the police

Composite: phrases or parts forming a legal definition of an offence (the composite of the definition of rape) Concurrent: existing or happening at the same time (see consecutive) Constraint: a thing that limits someone's freedom to do something (e.g. to choose); strict control over the way somebody behaves Contraceptive Sheath: a condom Corroborative evidence: evidence that supports the evidence of the victim Crown: a court of law (in England) which deals with criminal cases

Cunning us: the act of touching a woman's sexual organs with the mouth and tongue to give sexual pleasures. Defendant: a person in a court of law who is accused of committing a crime. DNA (Deoxyribonucleic Acid): The chemical in the cells of animal (and plants that carries genetic information and is a type of nucleic acid.

Duress: threats of force that are used to make somebody do something

Evidence: information that is used is a court of law to prove an accused guilty

Fellatio: the act of touching a man's penis with the lips and tongue to give sexual pleasure

Felony: a crime that is very serious (see misdemeanor) Forgery: making illegal copies of money or documents e.g. forged cheque

Frenulum: the membrane attaching the foreskin to the glans and shaft of the penis. It is richly supplied with the blood vessels and nerves. It is cut during circumcision. Grunt: to make a short low sound in the throat (especially pigs)

Indictment: the act of officially accusing someone with a crime.

Ingredient: one of the things needed to make something successful or complete (e.g. ingredient of rape)

Insensible: unconscious, unable to react to something Interrogate: to ask somebody a lot of questions for a long period of time

Jury: panel (of Judges; a group of people (members of the public and judges) who listen to the facts of the case before passing judgement

Labia: the lips that are found at the entrance to the woman's vagina

Malice aforethought: deliberate intention of committing a crime, usually murder

Misdemeanor: a crime that is considered not to be very serious (see below)

Misdirection: to give a jury wrong information about the law

Mitigation: lessening, alleviation, easing Obitter dicta: means other things which were said by a Judge Omission: failure to do something correctly.

In criminal law, an omission has to do with negligence of an individual, e.g. child neglecting. See an act. Overbear, overbearing: trying to control other people in unpleasant way; domineering. (Past tense is over borne) Perpetrator : doer; a person who commits a crime or does something that is wrong Persuasive case or precedent: a court's decision that is not decided in Zambia, Northern Rhodesia or commonwealth country, which a lower or equivalent court is likely to follow or obey the decision in it. (See binding case).

Predatory: using weaker people for one's own sexual advantage Prima facie: in Law, this is a good case with good evidence

Primary Offender: the actual perpetrator. In rape, it is the person who inserts his manhood into a woman. A secondary offender is an aide, abettor, procurer or counsellor

Principal Offender: a person who played a part in the commission of an offence

Proviso: it is a statutory defence that a magistrate has to explain to the accused when he pleads guilty to defilement.

Psychiatrist: a doctor who studies and treats mental illness

Psychotherapist: a person who treats mental illness by discussing one's problems rather than giving them drugs.

Quash: cancel; nullify; to officially say that a decision in a court of law is no longer valid or correct. It is to overrule case.

Ratio decidendi: the reason for the decision. It is the statement of law on which a judge based his decision. Ravish: to force a woman to have sex (rape, ravishment) Reckless ness: thoughtlessness; irresponsibility; showing lack of care about danger and the possible results of one's actions; very careless.

Sentence: punishment given by a court of law, e.g. a jail sentence

Sentencer: a magistrate or judge who give a sentence Sexual assault: an offence that is related to sexual intercourse, e.g. defilement, rape, etc. Statutory rape: defilement; the crime of having sex with somebody who is not legally old enough

Summing-up: a speech that the judge makes near the end of trial in a court of law, in which he reminds the jury (penal) about the evidence and the most important points in the case before the jury makes a decision Supposition: hypothesis; assumption; the act of believing that something is true even though it cannot be proved

Constraint: a thing that limits someone's freedom to do something (e.g. to choose); strict control over the way somebody behaves

Taunt: verbal abuse; an insulting or unkind remark to make someone angry

Thump: to beat strongly (e.g.) the heart thumps)

Trial: hearing of a case in court; a formal examination of evidence in court by a judge or magistrate to decide if the accused is guilty or not

Ultra vires: beyond one's powers

Uttering: presenting a forged document (e.g.cheque) to obtain a benefit (cash);

Utter: to say something

Verdict: a decision of the court on whether one is guilty or not

Vitiation of consent: lack of consent

Printed in the United States
By Bookmasters